MW00935090

BRICKS OF TRUTH

a book of aphorisms

by

Kenneth D. Rotar

Published by Dissident Press

ISBN-13: 978-1463754372

✳︎≋)(✦ ♌︎☐☐&;)(✦ ♦≋♏ ✦☐☐♎ ☐♐ ♌☐♎. And by writing this mystically coded statement, I have demonstrated how easy it is to scribe text and make it forever sacred.

This book is dedicated
to my wife, Mona,
whose love magicked me
from an "it" into a "he."

My thanks go to Peter Hamon, Patrick Julsing,
Sam Moen, Shane Parker, and Mona Rotar
for the use of their eyes and ears.

Preface

I

With few muscles to flex, I have had a wealth of time to flex my mind.

II

When I was courting Mona, trying to convince her that I would be a good spouse despite my disability, fate conspired with me: it kept giving her signs that I was the right man. Like magic, the good omens accumulated, prompting me to tease her about how the universe was dropping "bricks of truth" on her head to knock sense into it. I eventually won my case with this assistance, and I married Mona in 2001, ten happy years ago.

III

By putting together enough high-grade bricks, we can build an entire structure that can endure the huffing, puffing, and blowing of any brute.

IV

Even when I was still able to move my hands, I never enjoyed putting jigsaw puzzles together—except on one occasion. When

I was 13, my brother found a Playboy puzzle. We reassembled it as quickly as we could. Though many of the small pieces managed to titillate us, we knew that the whole picture would be greater than the sum of its parts. This book of aphorisms should not be much different.

V

Unlike a certain claim uttered by Sen. Jon Kyl that was patently inaccurate, each of my comments in this book was "intended to be a factual statement." That is, I did not lie to make my points.

VI

Since the integrity of my conceptual structure collapses if this book shelters factual errors, I have meticulously *re*verified all the information in it. Still, if you ever doubt anything I have written, *I beg you to google it*. The effort will be worthwhile, for you will end up unearthing more knowledge than I had room to include within aphorisms.

VII

I meant this book to be a good sampler platter of many thoughts. If some of them whet your appetite, you should treat yourself to larger portions—which many places serve. Always remember that a gluttonous brain is a healthy brain.

VIII

Friedrich Nietzsche correctly noted that "an aphorism, properly stamped and molded, has not been 'deciphered' when it has simply been read; rather, one has then to begin its exegesis." On this topic, he later drafted another remark: "I am brief; my readers themselves must become long and comprehensive in order to bring up and together all that I have thought, and thought deep down." *To grasp the complete value of an aphorism, the reader must work as hard as the writer did.* Do not let this book intimidate you, though, for it is a gentler taskmaster than Nietzsche's writings ever were (and for studying my aphorisms, you will be paid nearly as much cash as I am earning for writing them).

IX

Jo Godwin expressed a widespread belief of librarians: "A truly great library contains something in it to offend everyone." For a single book, I pray the same logic applies. My smorgasbord of 1000 aphorisms will surely cause all readers to frown at times — but by pulling no punches, I made this book as solid as I could.

X

I am a big fan of *Seinfeld*. Hardly a day goes by for me without some event triggering a memory of a scene from the show. I hope a similar thing happens in your daily life with the aphorisms in this collection.

1

In the Revolutionary War, many Americans who were not loyalists or patriots found their allegiances flip-flopping. Every time a new army occupied a town, the indifferent citizens would quickly become fair-weather fans, welcoming with open arms the change of guard. Nonetheless, as soon as their self-centered fantasies of improved fortune waned, so too did their fidelity. And thus was born the independent voter.

2

If humanity someday encounters other *intelligent* beings, will we merit the same recognition from them?

3

Regarding the stock market, Al Capone said, "It's a racket. Those stock market guys are crooked." For making this observation, Al should have won the Nobel Prize in Economic Sciences.

4

Balanced journalism unbalances truth. The theatrical routine of presenting multiple sides of every issue often proves deceptive; for example, by airing a contrary voice to the topic of "2 + 2 = 4," we give absurdity a plausible face. And with each fabricated debate, society's doubt-induced catatonia worsens.

5

Money cannot buy love, but it sure helps seal the deal.

6

If we were all as perfect as we contend to be in job interviews, our world would be a utopia.

7

From 1920 to 1933, our country declared war on alcohol. This period of prohibition brought us mafia and gang violence, high incarceration rates, racketeering, bootlegging, harder liquor, and increased consumption. *Now, with our war on drugs, we have déjà vu.*

8

Wrongdoers championed our taboo against tattling. *So why are we taking moral instructions from them?*

9

As we continue elevating "belief in something" ever higher above "knowledge of something," the Four Horsemen ride ever closer.

10

Once a public program is privatized, all checks and balances— other than private profit—are eliminated.

11

A democratic government that enforces the will of consumers via regulations is a legitimate participant in all free markets.

12

The most common form of suicide is by neglecting one's talents.

13

Self-affirmation is Cupid's truest arrow.

14

As a religion lays claim to the virtuous deeds of its followers, so too should it bear the burden of their *immoral* deeds (and the weightiest misdeeds are not those of the flock, but those of the shepherds). Until both Christianity and Islam accept some of the blame for acts done in their names, evil will keep flourishing.

15

Tea Partiers beware: you might actually get what you demand.

16

Without some form of afterlife, our exposure to history is but a bitter tease. It is like walking in late to see the finest play ever made —*The Story of Everything*. At first, fellow viewers fill you in on what you have missed with sketchy and subjective whisperings. You then settle back and watch the amazing tale unfold. Its plotlines increasingly ensnare you, holding you spellbound. Then suddenly, just as you become fully caught up in the play, the ushers cast you out of the theater! And never do you learn how it all ends.

17

Our body of scientific knowledge is expanding exponentially. As it is absorbed into the public consciousness, many religions that refuse to assimilate basic science will see their memberships shrink. Moreover, those who remain with the flocks will possess beliefs that are only a bit more evolved than "witches are among us" and "the universe revolves around Earth."

18

The ability to generalize is one of humanity's greatest survival tools. Its bad reputation arises from its misuse and overuse.

19

As Uncle Sam presses us to sacrifice for our nation, he entitles capitalists to hoard from it—and salutes *their* patriotism.

20

The quicker that oil companies extract our reserves, the quicker that our reserves disappear. Would it not be wiser to keep some in the bank?

21

With acts of creation that involve humanity and God—which came first, the chicken or the egg?

22

"Free market capitalism" is nothing but a euphemism for economic anarchy: the freer the markets, the more they resemble the Wild West.

23

If you want your children to learn good Christmas values, do not take them to Santa Claus; rather, take them to a soup kitchen to feed the hungry.

24

Even as fear of death keeps us from dying, fear of life keeps us from living.

25

Why are we shocked every time our idols fail to live up to the moral standards of our society? After all, their improprieties are to be expected: *until we value character more than fame, we will keep admiring the wrong individuals*. Consequently, when an idol does fall short as a role model, we must accept a considerable portion of the blame for having set the stage for the public fiasco.

26

If you have minimal love of knowledge, you should never become a teacher—no matter how smart you are.

27

A robot follows a program and lacks a conscience. Corporations are no different. All of their programs are fundamentally the same, centering on maximization of profits—and any acts of compassion carried out while executing such programs are just attempts to divert attention as the machines plunder.

28

Leaders seeking public support for military conquest seldom need to search farther than their local houses of worship. Holy wars always sell.

29

Unregulated capitalism is institutionalized class warfare.

30

A woman cannot free her life of shit as long as she continues to date assholes.

31

A corporation of laborers (i.e., a union) and a union of owners (i.e., a corporation) are equally legitimate. The purpose of both is to magnify the power of the individual market participants. If we sanction one of these alliances, we must sanction the other to maintain economic balance.

32

Go to a university to get knowledge, not merely a diploma. This everyday parchment verifies little more than one's capability to learn. Hence, students who accept a diploma as their sole prize have robbed themselves: it is often as worthless as wallpaper — whereas knowledge is always priceless.

33

If we are to maintain "a government of laws, and not of men," as John Adams and our other founders envisioned, the proper conduct of lawmakers and enforcement officials is vital. They must obey the laws that they administer or their hypocrisies will erode the foundations of government. Therefore, to protect the essential credibility of these public servants, we must hold them to a near-zero tolerance standard with severe penalties. *When they break the law, they should submit to the law — thereby setting an example for all.*

34

The most dangerous criminals are corrupt cops: their offenses do the additional harm of undermining our legal system. But who watches these watchmen? *Our police are too busy covering up one another's misdeeds, enforcing their Blue Code of Silence.* And so, we must eradicate this code by criminalizing it. Any officer who actively or passively assists in covering up the wrongdoings of a coworker should share the coworker's punishment. Furthermore, we should encourage, reward, and protect *all* whistleblowers.

35

The first big test of many relationships comes when you finally realize that your partner's feet really do not smell like roses.

36

If two children are playing and one misbehaves, blaming both equally is as ineffective as blaming neither. This is just as true when dealing with two political parties.

37

New lovers face a dilemma: by questioning romantic feelings too little, an emotion posing as love may come to deceive them; by questioning such feelings too much, genuine love may wither from suspicion.

38

When I was only nine months old, my parents learned that I had spinal muscular atrophy, a form of muscular dystrophy. Even though it was unlikely that I would live much past my teen years, they raised me no differently than my brothers and sister. Now, as I write this at the age of 45, I can barely move any of my limbs or digits, *but I am healthier and happier than ever*. My formula for wellbeing is to stay positive, keep busy, and heed my body's needs (naturally, having a loving wife and two adorable puppies also helps).

39

If you are fighting to prevent a woman from having an abortion, forcing her to bear the baby, at least be civilized enough to fight just as passionately for the formation of a society where this "child of God" will not suffer in poverty.

40

A world where everybody works only for individual self-interest with no concern for others versus one where everybody is equal and works together for the common good. Which of these two worlds sounds more like the realm of God? (Here is a hint: it is not the capitalistic one.)

41

Public assistance programs offer the needy too little for wellbeing, too much to turn down, and just enough to make revolution an unpalatable option.

42

American freedom and equality are dying. Wage slavery and class inequity are thriving. Put differently, *capitalism is poisoning democracy*. If we cannot reconcile these "sacred" doctrines—if one must perish—which of them will we rally to support?

43

Since ignorance is the ultimate cause of every ill, education is the ultimate curative program.

44

Police who do not first police themselves are not really police.

45

The most common Republican reply to a Democrat's valid criticism is "I know you are, but what am I?"

46

The corporate media is aiding the GOP by promoting the false impression that all of our politicians are equally corrupt and self-serving: conservatives who embrace this falsehood end up using it to rationalize voting repeatedly for Republicans, while liberals who embrace it end up using it to rationalize voting for no one.

47

"I could give a flying crap about the political process," Glenn Beck, the professed "rodeo clown," told *Forbes* magazine. "We're an entertainment company." It is alarming that a "news" network can empower a person with such a mind-set—granting him a forum to exploit public fears and to inflame anger, hatred, and violence. He is not trying to communicate political truths with his rabble-rousing rhetoric. Instead, he is using theatrics to rake in cash. This is enough to make one weep—without even a drop of Beck's agent for crocodile tears, Vicks VapoRub.

48

Wal-Mart is the whipping boy for corporate America. To the glee of jealous rivals, Wal-Mart takes lashes for the misdeeds of all corporations—even in cases where its siblings bear more of the blame.

49

Conservative politicians have a challenging job: day-after-day, they must sell their philosophy of selfishness.

50

To overcome fear of death, plan to live to a ripe old age; then, until you reach that age, allay your fears by reminding yourself that when death at last knocks, you will be more than ready.

51

The 14th Amendment led to corporations winning the status of real humans. These "golems" then accepted many of our privileges but few of our responsibilities. So, given that we have egregiously spoiled our corporate offspring, how can any one of us now be surprised to learn that they have grown up to become antisocial gangsters?

52

Greedy financiers are tempted to defraud just as greedy citizens are tempted to steal. Permitting the former to self-regulate is as reckless as permitting the latter to self-police.

53

When Ayn Rand argued her case for "full, pure, uncontrolled, unregulated *laissez-faire* capitalism," she asserted that market participants behave rationally. But this was a false premise: in reality, a significant portion of market behavior is a product of greed, an *ir*rational drive.

54

I graduated *magna cum laude*, earning a BBA degree in accounting (with a minor in philosophy) from the University of Wisconsin-Whitewater—which at that time had one of the finest accounting programs in the nation. So I will now use my education to sum up *every* Republican budget proposal: if we will simply agree to keep cutting the taxes of our aristocrats, each of us will someday get our very own pony!

55

When President George W. Bush left office, America was 232 years old and over $10 trillion in debt. Bush and his dad, along with Ronald Reagan, were responsible for more than 75% of this amount. Does this make the GOP the *"borrow* and spend" party?

56

Religious leaders should encourage humans to be humans rather than sheep.

57

Too often, the act of a person giving professional counseling to a client echoes that of the blind leading the blind.

58

Most religious groups are just pushy street gangs that loiter in swankier hangouts.

59

A note to religious institutions: you do not have a monopoly on morality.

60

Without doubt, the avid readers of the German Reich's *Völkischer Beobachter* ("People's Observer") and the Soviet Union's *Pravda* ("Truth") praised these patriotic newspapers for being "fair and balanced."

61

Gone are the indecent days of businesspeople sleeping with their regulators. Nowadays, they are all happily married to one another —*with the next generation of free market babies on board.*

62

Step into a tavern and you are likely to see Fox News playing on the TVs. *Drugs always help with brainwashing.*

63

The belief that "all men are sexist" is sexist—and the belief that "all white people are racist" is racist.

64

Of all supervillains, one stands out as the most diabolical. He uses his genius intellect—the fusion of many brains—to seize control of everything in the world. Laws mean little to him and morality means even less. When necessary, he can clone any part of himself at will. Those whom he cannot defeat, he bribes with his immense wealth. No one can reason with him or slay him, and no prison can hold him. His alter ego is a charitable, patriotic, god-fearing, law-abiding entrepreneur. The public idolizes him, granting him every wish. He owns the politicians. And his name is Mr. Corporation.

65

After the financial crash of 2008, Alan Greenspan confessed that his free market philosophy was fundamentally flawed: "I made a mistake in presuming that the self-interest of organizations, specifically banks and others, were such that they were best capable of protecting their own shareholders and their equity in the firms."

Despite this statement, free market ideologues are still defending their sacred cow, contending that it was *too many regulations* that caused the crisis. They are pressuring us for even freer markets. *But can we really afford another one of their "mistakes"?*

66

In a culture where a good number of men are willing to do almost anything to win the affections of a woman, who is then the most powerful?

67

If run-of-the-mill Tea Partiers could conceal themselves beneath white sheets, would they at last find the courage to voice their *true* convictions?

68

The mess in Waco illustrated what happens when bullies with guns meet nutcases with guns.

69

Market regulations serve purposes besides inhibiting fraud. One of these is to provide financial information that people need in order to make prudent market decisions. How many investors now wish that stricter reporting standards for derivatives had been in place prior to the 2008 financial meltdown?

70

For decades, single-issue, pro-life voters have sworn allegiance to the Republican Party in exchange for its disingenuous promise to ban abortions. Their pact has empowered conservative agendas that have destroyed family incomes, starved children, sacrificed the uninsured sick, criminalized millions of nonviolent drug users, executed innocent prisoners, waged senseless wars that killed countless civilians, and poisoned our surroundings. *Is this what we call "making a deal with the devil"?*

71

Detractors of socialized programs would gain credibility if they did not idolize the world's most costly socialized program: the United States military. It would be quite feasible to privatize all military-related functions, with financing provided by those of us who feel most threatened by foreign nations. Yes, many will rightly argue that military matters are too critical to place in the hands of private industry—just as anybody who is dying from lack of access to medical treatment will rightly argue that health insurance matters are too critical to place in the same hands.

72

Reaganomics is a failed religion. Ronnie's merry men robbed the lower and middle classes to assist the rich, swearing the wealth would trickle down. It did not. The rich now own far more than ever. So why are they not making things? They are not doing so because the "trickled on" lower classes have too little cash and credit left to buy stuff. This dilemma will get worse: further production cuts will lead to higher unemployment, poorer buyers, and even more production cuts—a perpetual spiral down to ruin. *Ronald Reagan's worshippers should halt their deification efforts while the world assesses the costs of his class warfare.*

73

For over 30 years, the plutocracy has robbed us with its "trickle-down" economics—and this reverse Robin Hood system of class warfare has financially crippled our nation. Hence, it is time for us to institute a more sensible and equitable policy, one that will restore our middle class. Put simply, we need a healthy dose of "trickle-*up*" economics.

74

As you become more intimate with death, you become more intimate with life.

75

Sarah Palin asked the supporters of President Obama, "How's that hopey, changey stuff workin' out for ya?" Considering the disasters he inherited, it is working out as well as we could have expected. The only noteworthy "hope" that died was the one centered on the GOP making a "change" that would have put our nation's interests before its own. Tell us, Sarah, how is the GOP's hope for Obama's failure (i.e., America's failure) working out?

76

If we mandate that everyone, rich and poor, rely exclusively on the services of randomly assigned public defenders, we will gain the necessary motivation to deal with the unfairness in our criminal justice system. *Only after the wealthy can no longer purchase their justice will they at last consider granting it to all.*

77

Operation Northwoods was an unexecuted plan drafted by the Joint Chiefs of Staff in 1962. It proposed staged assaults that would frame Cuba—mustering domestic and global support for launching a war. These proposed "assaults" included blowing up a U.S. ship, shooting down a counterfeit civilian airliner, sinking a refugee boat, and conducting terrorist attacks on American soil. If our leaders could recommend this false flag operation, *they can most certainly implement a similar plan whenever so desired.*

78

A perfect being can see through ruses, so dismiss the temptation of Jesus in the desert. A perfect being is fearless, so dismiss the agony of Jesus in the Garden of Gethsemane. A perfect being can ignore pain, so dismiss the sacrifice of Jesus on the cross. Or we could just give Jesus credit for his struggles by dismissing the fish story of his perfection.

79

If law enforcement agencies continue to fail in preventing *every* felony, should we offer our police more support, helping them to improve—or should we terminate them for being big failures? Using the illogic of deregulators, all law enforcement officials would promptly be sent home (and our government would be so much smaller and nicer).

80

In 2009, Glenn Beck claimed that he states "on the air all [the] time, 'if you take what I say as gospel, you're an idiot.'" And so I now give him this century's "Truth-in-Advertising Award."

81

Instead of citizens using the media to inform politicians of public wants, politicians use the media to inform citizens of what the public *should* want. The media must nurture closer ties with the mouths of citizens and the ears of politicians.

82

The same people who condemn our government's actions at Waco get joyously aroused by our government's routine torture and killing of foreigners without due process. These hypocrites deserve the same rights as they would give to the least of their brethren.

83

We once had a wise, peaceful leader, invested with integrity and intelligence—but we dismissed President Jimmy Carter after just one term. For this unworthy act, we have earned every immoral politician that fate has since sent us. They are the wages of our sin.

84

The choice between Republicans and Democrats is a choice between corporate welfare and individual welfare. Besides exploring the ethical issues, we must determine which of these "redistribution of wealth" strategies will stimulate our economy the most. The answer is now clearer than ever: we should enhance the buying power of lower- and middle-class individuals—thereby spurring demand for corporate goods and services.

85

A healthy democracy requires a well-informed electorate; without it, tyranny prevails. Hence, the most treacherous threat to our country may be the prevailing campaign to reward ignoramuses while mocking intellectuals. Did we learn nothing from *Revenge of the Nerds*?

86

Undocumented immigrants are modern-day slaves. But given that they serve "voluntarily," their employers (i.e., masters) can mistreat them while dodging the disagreeable label of slaveholder. And as the demonized slaves take the blame for accepting the covert work invitations, the conniving masters prosper because Uncle Sam routinely turns a blind eye to their exploitative operations.

87

The press should be reporting news—not instigating "news."

88

I live in Madison, Wisconsin, one of the most progressive cities in America. Madison also consistently rates as one of America's best cities to live in. *This is not a coincidence.*

89

Both Democrats and Republicans commit sexual improprieties—but only one party hypocritically campaigns as the champion of "family values."

90

Perhaps "GOP" stands for "Gotcha on Placebos": Republicans keep awarding the real tax breaks, opportunities, and freedoms to the aristocrats while the rest of us get hyped-up placebos.

91

The GOP claims that it stands for limited government. This is a half-truth (i.e., half-lie): the GOP wants a limited government *only* for corporations and the affluent. For everybody else, the party works to restrict freedoms, dictate morality, and imprison without restraint—all to enforce order on the rabble. The GOP will not allow us to disturb the liberties of our betters.

92

When dealing with complex social issues, simple knee-jerk solutions are seldom correct. However, this rarely stops ignorant people from preaching about these "commonsense" solutions.

93

The healthiest Americans are the engorged corporate parasites of our healthcare system.

94

Each time you get out of bed for the day, you are choosing (most often unconsciously) *to live*. Such daily denials of suicide add great value to our existence—and only when we lose the ability to choose due to infirmity do we come to appreciate its importance.

95

Social liberals counter social conservatives, and Jesus counters Satan. Jesus is a social liberal. Therefore, Satan is a....

96

Not all conspiracy theories are equal: a few are actually factual. Nevertheless, with swarms of bogus theories encircling us, the genuine ones get lost in the chaff—a situation that is appreciated and cultivated by conspirators. *The more voices that cry wolf, the more we ignore every voice.*

97

The Catholic Church really must stop recruiting its priests from the membership of Spanky's He-Man Woman Haters Club.

98

In 1997, several individuals who would soon serve in President Bush's administration—including Dick Cheney, Don Rumsfeld, and Paul Wolfowitz—created a think tank called Project for the New American Century. Three years later, the group published

Rebuilding America's Defenses. It called for the transformation of our military, noting that the process "is likely to be a long one, absent some catastrophic and catalyzing event—like a new Pearl Harbor." Twelve months later, on September 11, 2001, they got their "new Pearl Harbor"—and *everything* fell into place.

99

The mother of all conspiracies is the 9/11 cover-up. About half of American citizens believe our government was duplicitous with the attacks, and reams of incriminating documents are available (e.g., www.historycommons.org [the *Complete 911 Timeline*] and www.911proof.com). The evidence is there for those who are not too trusting, too frightened, or too lazy to look. Some people will pass me off as merely another "conspiracy nut," but those who do so *without even examining the evidence* are betraying the victims of 9/11.

100

A month after 9/11, Bush's administration railroaded the Patriot Act through Congress. Two Senate Democrats, Majority Leader Tom Daschle and Judiciary Committee Chairman Patrick Leahy, held key positions that could block or slow the bill—and they had voiced concerns regarding its many constitutional problems. The debate had scarcely begun when two lawmakers received anthrax in the mail—Daschle and Leahy. *The short-lived anthrax operation directly targeted no other individuals.* The message was quiet but clear: pass the Patriot Act—or else.... Again, Bush and Cheney got just the "coincidence" that they needed to carry out their power grab.

101

Just as espionage novels can dupe the shrewdest of us, so too can powerful people—and only exhaustive research can enable us to see through their deceptions. The morsels that our mainstream media feeds us are untrustworthy: conspirators can easily flavor any of them. Consequently, to be effective patriots, we must dig much deeper.

102

The revolutionaries that run our militias have one major defect: their proposed cures are far more noxious than the diseases they allegedly treat.

103

If papal officials continue to act like self-serving politicians when handling church scandals, we should impeach the pope and all of his party men.

104

It is sad that convicts seem to have better moral compasses than Catholic leaders do: in prisons, child molesters are the lowest of the low, and their peers always chastise them accordingly.

105

One capitalist's gambling shop is another capitalist's marijuana dispensary is another capitalist's investment bank. The primary difference between these types of businesses is that free market investment brokers almost never go to prison—even when their shady deals wipe out the life savings of thousands of victims.

106

Tea Partiers are like blind hunters gunning for beasts: though they occasionally have the right targets in mind, they will most often shoot in the wrong direction.

107

The apologies of a Wall Street executive are as worthless as the apologies of a serial burglar who got away scot-free.

108

There is little hope to impede treacheries like the Iraq War and the Wall Street bailout as long as our media continues to assist conspirators in assassinating our whistleblowers.

109

Anyone can tear down solutions, but few can build them.

110

In a master-slave business arrangement, who is really the taker and who is really the maker? (Now note that the answer to this question does not change even in cases where the master offers the slave a small portion of the profits.)

111

Lower- and middle-class Republicans are the Confederate soldiers of today: although they own almost no wealth (i.e., no slaves), they sacrifice their interests to struggle for the free markets (i.e., the rights) of the aristocrats (i.e., the slaveholders)—all so that the rich can get richer from continued exploitation. And as before, the moneygrubbers infect Johnny Reb with patriotic fever so that few soldiers will ever question their role as pawns.

112

The Confederate flag never really symbolized a rebellion against a domineering national government. Instead, the flag symbolized the hypocritical replacement of a domineering government with an even more domineering one that set aristocratic licenses above everybody else's unalienable rights to life, liberty, and the pursuit of happiness.

113

In the Iraq and Afghanistan Wars, why did Bush privatize so many tasks that our military had traditionally performed with greater security and efficiency and lower costs? Perhaps he preferred contractors because they could always kick back a little love for their succulent deals. Or maybe it was because they could carry out the naughty work (e.g., "enhanced" interrogations), thereby disconnecting the White House from accountability. Whatever the reasons, Cheney's old company, Halliburton, now crowns the long historical list of traitorous war profiteers.

114

The myth of a liberal media bias should have forever died when the press—after having persecuted Bill Clinton for getting a blowjob —did little but look away while George W. Bush sodomized the world.

115

Left-wing socialism is now less of a threat than right-wing fascism.

116

Rather than simply informing us of product availability, most of today's advertising is brainwashing us into spending money we do not have on crap we do not need. Never underestimate the influence of "persuasive" marketing: its prevalence is evidence of its power. It is an insidious threat to our liberty that we must soon address.

117

Across the world, free market capitalists use America's soldiers as their hit men. No matter how inhumanely an unregulated company exploits Third World citizens, we praise its entrepreneurialism. Then, if the oppressed people fight for their rights, the profiteers condemn them as narco-traffickers, terrorists, or Marxists—and before long, we dutifully kill the "troublemakers" in one of our never-ending wars on drugs, terror, and communism.

118

America is like a rich, bratty schoolboy who is totally clueless as to why so many of his peers hate him. Instead of immediately beating or shunning them, would it not be wiser for the child to try to understand the causes of their resentment? Some national introspection might spare us a few growing pains.

119

Though their followers will deny it, communism and free market capitalism both succumb to the same Kryptonite: uninhibited greed.

120

It is Christian fundamentalists, not Islamic, that we must worry about. Although both camps cultivate hatred of our society, it is our home-brewed extremists that have infiltrated *every* corner of America's government to enforce their theocratic will.

121

Big business can bribe both Republican and Democratic politicians. However, it is unnecessary to do so with Republicans, for they already lick the boots of big business.

122

God probably wanted to enlighten us about topics such as the big bang and evolution in the Book of Genesis, but he knew he needed a simple story for the simple minds of yesterday—and today.

123

If somebody coerced you to play Russian roulette with a ten-shot revolver, how much would you give to remove the one bullet? How much would you give if your spouse or children were in the game? Now, imagine there is an identical 10% chance that global warming is real and that it will gravely harm billions of people, including you and your loved ones. How much would you give to take *this* "bullet" out of play?

124

Corporate regulators are like defanged cobras: they try to look intimidating, but they have no bite and most executives know how to charm them.

125

Waste and fraud defile public and private sector entities alike. The private ones look cleaner only because they are not required to reveal their dirt as openly. It is easier to love people who can mask most of their blemishes.

126

If I received a dollar for every time I caught Rush Limbaugh and his ilk misrepresenting the facts, I would vote Republican. How else could I shape America's tax policy to shelter my newfound megabucks?

127

It is usually difficult to talk facts with people of faith owing to their dependency on belief instead of reason. Hence, the ever-strengthening merger of the GOP and the Christian right has made it equally toilsome to talk facts with most Republicans. Dogma has replaced logical debate as the pilot of our nation.

128

For the countless laborers who live paycheck to paycheck, every financial decision—regardless of the amount of cash involved— is risky. No billionaires can honestly make the same claim. *So when will capitalists begin rewarding these laborers for being the true risk takers in our economy?*

129

Treating independent political expenditures by corporations and unions as a constitutionally protected form of speech *that cannot be limited* is like permitting persons who own diamond-studded megaphones to falsely shout "fire" in a crowded theatre to cause a panic—even as the rest of us are still forbidden to do so.

130

One can see the tyranny of Tea Partiers in their new math: they claim majority rule even when they have only 30% of the votes.

131

Your mind mirrors your media consumption.

132

George W. Bush's legacy is global posttraumatic stress disorder.

133

Do not get overly impressed by someone's profession. After all, 50% of all people in any particular field finished in the bottom half of their class.

134

Accusing the poor of "class warfare" is like accusing a woman of domestic abuse when she pushes her husband in self-defense after having passively suffered through many years of spousal beatings.

135

The GOP is always too gutless to admit ideological opposition to bills for populist reforms. Instead, it discredits them, saying that they do too little or too much. It then claims that it has superior plans. Of course, these are simply vague variations on the same theme: uphold the status quo. By using this strategy, Republicans can kill constructive legislation without ever appearing to be ogres.

136

I see a Christian, I see a Muslim—they seem much alike—and I am hopeful. I see a Christian fundamentalist, I see an Islamic fundamentalist—they seem much alike—and I am terrified.

137

The label "independent voter" gives cover to a menacing group of ignoramuses: low-information voters. Because of their large numbers, when they *flip* with the wind, America *flops*—whether it is good for us or not. Our fortunes rest on the whims of people who get their political insights primarily from *American Idol*.

138

Given that Third World poverty breeds terrorists, and America is losing its own war against poverty, what realistic hope is there to curb terrorism by exporting our flawed brand of capitalism?

139

A Christian who overly fears death is not much of a Christian.

140

Though we will use executions to end the lives of people who do not want to die, we will not use physician-assisted suicide to end the lives of people who *do* want to die. In other words, *we do not truly value life*; rather, we value cold-blooded contrariness.

141

Painkillers befuddle your mind, saliva chokes your windpipe, and feces soil your diapers. Some people will let such degradations happen to you in your final days so that they may keep you "alive" as long as possible. I denounce these people for being controlling, uncompassionate monsters. *If we do not actively practice assisted suicide, we are then passively practicing assisted torture.*

142

There is absolutely no slippery slope between physician-assisted suicide and murder: the former comes at the explicit request of the patient; the latter does not.

143

My end-of-life choices are always between me and my god, not you and yours.

144

Do not force me to endure prolonged suffering at the end of life just to gratify your morbid desire for a "heroic" role model. I do not live or die for your sake *unless I so choose*. And if you cannot overcome your need for an idol, a shrink can help.

145

Most opponents of physician-assisted suicide will join the other team once they begin to experience their own terminal torture.

146

Wall Street is operating shell games with financial derivatives. Their built-in complexities serve to deceive any "marks" who do not have Einsteinian intellects. Since even our "cops" cannot decipher these games, *extraordinary disclosure rules are necessary*.

147

Debating public policy with a religious person is as frustrating as reasoning with a willful child who has an imaginary pal. One quickly tires of composing unheeded rebuttals for every instance that the child screams, "But my friend says...!"

148

The underlying law of capitalism: wealth begets wealth, poverty begets poverty.

149

Through the ever-increasing privatization of all of our natural resources, we commoners are beginning to get a taste of what it was like for Native Americans to be forced onto reservations.

150

America's government classifies sensitive information into three categories (confidential, secret, and top secret) to indicate the degree of damage that unauthorized disclosure would cause to our national security. *So which of these files in particular do our bureaucrats use to bury information concerning their embarrassing and illegal acts?*

151

The only true libertarian is a lone hunter-gatherer.

152

Banks should be the means, not the ends, of a healthy economy.

153

Concentrated wealth begets concentrated power begets plutocracy —rule by the wealthy. This has always been the primary threat to our democracy, only kept in check by unrelenting efforts to empower our poorest citizens. *Even though the wealthy may hold all the aces, we must stay in the game by holding on to the rest of the deck.*

154

When a person sues a corporation, we call the lawsuit frivolous. On the other hand, when a corporation sues a person, we call the lawsuit "smart business."

155

Even when the law is not on a corporation's side, it is still the odds-on favorite to win any legal battles: it can incessantly beat most opponents into submission with its gang of staff lawyers.

156

Republican tax cuts for the wealthy lead to budget deficits, which lead to program cuts, which lead to budget surpluses, which lead to further Republican tax cuts for the wealthy — thereby renewing the GOP budget cycle for the development of destabilizing class inequalities and an ineffectual government.

157

The GOP is extremely busy saving our nation from boogeymen (e.g., the abortionists, the atheists, the black people, the liberal elite, the homosexuals, the drug addicts, the environmentalists, the feminists, the communists, the felons, the welfare queens, the pacifists, the unionists, the Muslims, the Mexicans, the socialists, the progressives, the terrorists). With so many scary persons to shield us from, how can we dare to criticize Republicans for not having enough time or energy left to produce legislation that will actually *improve* America?

158

In a perfect world, the GOP would protect us from Tea Partiers.

159

It may be true that most journalists lean to the left, but it is also undeniably true that most of their corporate bosses lean to the right. So who do you *honestly* think owns the final say over the general political slant of a business's news coverage?

160

Under Islamic sharia law, a woman can prove rape only by getting her assailant to confess or by producing four Muslim males who witnessed it (civilized people usually know these witnesses by another name: *accomplices*). If she cannot "prove" her case, the court will convict her of fornication or adultery, depending on her marital status. The penalty for fornication is a hundred lashes and banishment; for adultery, men bury the rape victim up to the chest in sand and slowly stone her to a bloody pulp. And this is but a sample of Islamic justice! *We must never tolerate religions that tolerate such Dark Age barbarities.*

161

Since defendants seldom take the stand in court, *police officers are the default champions of perjury.* Many will say *anything* to seal a conviction or to cover-up improper procedures.

162

Wall Street derivatives brokers are corrupt bookies who take *and place* bets on sports teams that they secretly manage.

163

In 2006, the GOP sneaked into law the Unlawful Internet Gambling Enforcement Act. The act mainly starves online gambling sites by cutting off wire transfers. America is one of only a few countries with such a regulation. But of more interest, *the act specifically exempts trading in securities and like instruments.* How much extra evidence do we need to prove that the GOP desires freedom for the aristocrats and subjugation for us commoners?

164

A poor person's wager is a rich person's investment; or in other words, a poor person's regulated financial transaction is a rich person's *unregulated* financial transaction. As is typically the case, governmental intrusion is tolerable only when it infringes upon the rights of poor people.

165

Las Vegas casinos persuade you to visit, not for your wellbeing, *but so that they can "play" with your money*. Now why would Wall Street casinos want you to bring in your Social Security funds?

166

The more money the public pumps into stocks, the bigger the bull market. But when the flow of money dries up, the market stabilizes and yields leaner prospects for "players" to game the system. Hence, they pressure us to put in all of our funds and to stay invested even when the market crashes. Over many years, we *might* receive a good return, but nothing close to the fortunes made by players riding the market waves *we* create. Moreover, for each dollar of profit the players game out of the system, we lose a dollar from *our* worth. Do not be deceived: your cash is Wall Street's toy.

167

A society that puts more faith in groundhogs than in scientists is doomed to eternal winter.

168

The surest gateway to hard drugs is drug testing. Urine, blood, and saliva tests can detect marijuana for over a month, but most hard drugs and alcohol for only a few days. Given the frequency of testing for job applicants and probationers, which drugs will these people turn to more often?

169

As real Christians look to the New Testament for guidance, fake Christians look to the Old Testament for ammunition.

170

It would be easier for a Christian to be Christlike if ministers would teach exclusively from the New Testament, shelving the Old Testament within the "history" section of their libraries.

171

I am beginning to believe that "GOP" is actually an acronym for "Grand Ostrich Party." If Republicans cannot "fix" a problem by cutting the aristocracy's taxes, deregulating corporations, blowing up someone, or restricting liberties of the rabble, they merely bury their heads in the sand as ostriches do (in myth)—praying that the problem does not really exist or that it will just go away if it is ignored long enough.

172

Pure free market capitalism is a theoretical impossibility: every market transaction stands on a foundation of essential rules and regulations. Capitalists simply use the concept of free markets to persuade us to eliminate laws that they do not like.

173

If free market capitalism is all about freedom, how do we explain the prevalence of forced labor throughout much of the history of American capitalism?

174

There is a nightmare worse than being murdered: having citizens execute you for a murder you did not commit. Imagine your trial and its ruination of your name. Imagine your years of fruitless appeals. Imagine your final days surrounded by people rejoicing your death. No words can convey the passions felt in this hell.

175

Our criminal justice system operates on the principle that it is better for us to set ten guilty persons free than to convict one innocent person. Obviously, we must exercise additional caution with executions. So how should we proceed when studies estimate that 5% of the thousands on death row are in fact innocent?

176

At an execution, the condemned is seldom the most deranged monster present. That distinction usually goes to all the sickos who gleefully celebrate the event outside the prison walls.

177

In six years as governor of Texas, George W. Bush (together with his appointees to the Board of Pardons and Paroles) executed 152 people *while commuting only one sentence*. Although other states with far better legal systems are uncovering significant numbers of wrongly convicted people on death row, he insisted that all of the persons brought before him for execution had received full access to a fair trial and that it was not his place to overrule a jury (*actually*, it is). My first exposure to Bush was via an article I read in 2000 that described many of the contentious executions rubber-stamped on his watch. This prophetic exposé shed light on his intellectual laziness and contempt for human rights, *traits that would soon bring the entire world much distress.*

178

Amnesty International knows of 18 nations that executed people in 2009: Bangladesh, Malaysia, Yemen, Egypt, Iran, Iraq, Syria, Libya, North Korea, Botswana, Saudi Arabia, Singapore, China, Viet Nam, Thailand, Sudan, Japan, and America. All are from Africa or Asia, except for ours. *Do you like the company we are keeping?*

179

A long time ago, civilized societies trumped "an eye for an eye" with "two wrongs don't make a right."

180

If you condone our nation's practice of executing duly convicted criminals, how are you any different from those who condoned the execution of Jesus?

181

Though Lady Justice may be blind, she is clearly not *color*blind: she easily differentiates between white and nonwhite—and she always favors green.

182

Capital punishment is the ultimate in class warfare: if you are poor, you are executed; if you are rich, you are *O.J.ed*.

183

Not only do we execute some persons with cognitive disabilities, we also regularly execute persons who have public defenders with cognitive disabilities.

184

Given that it is virtually impossible to measure the positive or negative effects of the death penalty on murder rates, we should rely on commonsense analysis. Most murders are emotionally impulsive acts, so how many potential killers will take the time to weigh the risk of receiving a death sentence? It is implausible that any unhinged person would call a timeout to deliberate: "I would murder this fucker if I faced *merely* a life sentence. But since I *might* be caught and I *could* be executed, I am just going to peacefully walk away."

185

Owing to the gravity of an execution, we must earnestly question the credibility of *every* confession for a capital offense. Any suspect who gives one is obviously incompetent—or has been coerced or tricked. And just how reliable is any admission of guilt that arises from incompetence, coercion, or trickery? If we wish to put a person to death, let us base our judgment on concrete evidence, not the slop of mind games.

186

When a society embraces state-sanctioned executions, the public psyche subliminally absorbs two unintended messages: some human life is not sacred, and lethal revenge is acceptable.

187

I do not want murderers to contemplate their own deaths. I want them to contemplate their *victims'* deaths—for exceedingly long lifetimes.

188

As regards the survivors of murder victims, a psychiatrist—not an executioner—is best equipped to provide healthy closure.

189

A justice system without complete objectivity is unjust. Whenever a court permits the emotional survivors of a murder victim to sway sentencing toward either execution or life imprisonment, we lose objectivity. Hence, we must strive to base punishment solely on the crime, not on the strength of someone's thirst for a particular vengeance.

190

It is astonishing that those who most distrust the competency of our government are also the most likely to gullibly believe that it will *always* execute the correct person for a given crime.

191

If you support a gang that murders someone, you are an accessory to murder. When our government executes an innocent person, it is murder. So what are you if you support such an execution? I do believe that accessories to murder get fantastic seats in Hell.

192

When George W. Bush said, "We're fighting them there so we don't have to fight them here," a jubilant Osama bin Laden probably replied, "We're fighting them here because we can't fight them there. Checkmate, President Bush!"

193

Do not be afraid to admit you are wrong. Only gods are perfect.

194

On his show in 1995, Rush Limbaugh stated, "And so if people are violating the law by doing drugs, they ought to be accused and they ought to be convicted and they ought to be sent up." Then, when he was arrested on a felony charge connected to his many years of illegal narcotics use, he avoided being prosecuted by cutting a deal: in effect, he pleaded "*not* guilty" and continued his addiction treatment—and all charges and investigations were dropped. Although the prosecution asserted that it had enough evidence to support over 10 felony counts, his attorney argued, "The public is better served by treating addicts as patients rather than criminals." *Limbaugh received a "namby-pamby, liberal" deal!* Other addicts hardly ever get so much compassionate leniency, thanks to hard-asses like him: right-wingers incessantly badger the government into being tough on all crimes—*except their own.*

195

"The ocean will take care of this on its own if it was left alone and left out there," Rush Limbaugh said, trivializing the huge BP oil spill in the Gulf of Mexico. "It's natural. It's as natural as the ocean water is." I will expose this horseshit for those who are too dimwitted to detect it. But first, Rush, allow me to stir some crude oil into your glass of water. Don't worry, drink it down! It's as natural as your cold blood is—and even if it does kill you, worms will eventually take care of the mess on their own.

196

Where were all of the safety features, equipment, and plans that may have prevented BP's oil spill? They were not in place because Dick Cheney's oil cronies had hijacked the Minerals Management Service long ago, eliminating or weakening needed safety laws. *And as with the financial collapse from the deregulation of Wall Street, corporate gains become our losses.*

197

A corporation is not innately evil, but it lacks a moral compass and a conscience. Therefore, we must give it a code of ethics that our courts can enforce with severe legal punishments. If we do not do so, the unchecked thirst for profit will inevitably lead it to evildoings.

198

If a person takes a pile of shit and packages it under a "Flower Power" label, it is still just a pile of shit. Now, regarding the most recent repackaging of right-wing extremists under the "Tea Party" label....

199

A corporation has much more capacity than a lone person does to harm society; nonetheless, our laws target bunnies instead of wolf packs.

200

The principal objective of incorporating is to divorce authority from accountability. Within a corporate structure, officers can direct misdeeds that would bring incarceration or bankruptcy through fines to a sole proprietor. Not only is our legal system unable or unwilling to criminally charge corporate officers, it is also hesitant to assess warranted fines that may injure the entity, leading to layoffs. *This corporate authority without accountability fulfills the wet dreams of scoundrels (i.e., free market capitalists).*

201

If there is reincarnation, I hope I come back as a corporation.

202

To stay robust, capitalism must constantly evolve: bad business needs to die to make room for good business. When we permit an inefficient or antisocial corporation to persist, we degrade our capitalist system. Naturally, a sick corporation will struggle and bargain for its life, so we must resolutely carry out involuntary commercial euthanasia.

203

Libertarians are the descendants of southern slave owners: they are still greedily battling to place their own property rights over the human rights of others.

204

Corporations are blackmailing everybody: "Do not dare to punish us for our crimes, or we will pack and leave, ruining your local economies." Due to our fear of challenging such threats, we now treat *all* corporations as if they are "too big to fail."

205

America did not invent business. Entrepreneurs have created *and lost* businesses throughout human history, and will continue to do so long past the time that America vanishes from memory. With most businesses, there are few reasons for society to fear a failure: greed will swiftly fill all vacated market niches. Any economic pain will be short-lived and less damaging than the perpetuation of bad business. The sole exception to this analysis rises from the mega-corporations that are literally too big to fail, for we cannot let them die no matter how noxious they become. *Thus, to defend the vigorous evolution of capitalism, our government must hack these behemoths down to slayable sizes.*

206

Punishment is the surest way to deter the unconscionable actions of corporations. Our courts must hand out punitive fines to the moneymakers and prison sentences to the decision makers (usually they are the same people). The fines must be appreciably larger than the profit netted from an illegality — even if they lead to the financial ruination of a corporation or its profiteers. And as for assessing the culpability of the decision makers, we must reunite accountability with authority by incarcerating corporate generals for the crimes carried out by their foot soldiers.

207

Many corporations might possibly be "too big to fail" —but none of their executives can truthfully make the same claim.

208

As soon as we demonstrate to capitalists that they can no longer hide behind a corporate shield, most of them will at last try to self-regulate their antisocial behavior—and healthy capitalism will begin to enrich *all* citizens.

209

Burqas are nothing but glorified chastity belts for the wives of sexually insecure Muslim men.

210

We do not decrease our reliance on foreign oil by extracting our reserves: when a company drills our fields, the oil becomes its own to sell on the global market. We have no claim to this oil, and so we still end up getting all of ours from an international pool. Clearly, no one has tried to spell out this simple system with small enough words for our oil guru—Sarah Palin.

211

No sports teams would ever call themselves the Maggots, the Cripples, or the Slaughtering Nazis. Teams choose names that denote strength and pride—and such names then bestow honor back to their namesakes (i.e., the Seminoles, the Fighting Sioux, and the Redskins promote fan homage for Native Americans).

212

Sarah Palin will finally see what "death panels" really are when her disabled child, Trig, becomes a man: *every* health insurance company will deny him treatment, thereby sentencing him to death (unless, of course, our "socialist" government intervenes).

213

For-profit businesses will always strive to increase and expand demand by any means possible. Hence, only a foolish society will ever agree to privatize negative goods and services such as narcotics, incarceration, and warfare.

214

The more we equip the police with excuses to detain someone, the more the police will detain *every*one.

215

If you cannot muster the courage to candidly state your beliefs in public, perhaps you should not have them.

216

I suspect that many supporters of handgun rights would tone down their enthusiasm upon interviewing a sampling of *typical* handgun owners.

217

Countries around the world have nationalized most global oil and gas reserves, kicking out private companies. By doing so, these countries regained control of their reserves and related revenues. America could do the same, but why should we even bother? We could never hope to master the unique skill set of BP, ExxonMobil, and the other supermajors: they can take our reserves, gouge us on prices, and poison our environment—all for an obscenely high profit.

218

Among America's professors, historians, sociologists, economists, and anthropologists, registered Democrats substantially outnumber registered Republicans. *But what could all these brainiacs possibly know about how our world works?*

219

I would prefer that someone call me the "g-word" (i.e., gimp) to my face instead of behind my back.

220

If you want to keep Uncle Sam's hands off your religion, you had better keep your religion's hands off Uncle Sam.

221

Regarding our war on terror, mull over this rough formula: (*the number of civilians killed*) x (*the average number of persons who loved each victim*) = (*the number of new potential terrorists*).

222

Most Americans are libertarians at heart, backing the philosophy of individual liberty and limited government. But these like-minded people always come into conflict as soon as they begin listing their personal exceptions to this philosophy. Moreover, once we institutionalize all of the exceptions, we end up with a system that looks much like our current one.

223

"Indeed, I support a zero option for all nuclear arms. As I've said before, my dream is to see the day when nuclear weapons will be banished from the face of the Earth." Barack Obama did not make this "wimpy" declaration. Ronald Reagan did, in 1984.

224

In his first year as president, Ronald Reagan slashed taxes. He followed this up with three big tax hikes (1982 to 1984) and two modest ones (1985 and 1987). Over his eight years, the combined payroll and income tax rates for the average middle-class family with children actually *increased*. To be honest, Reagan's record of tax cuts seems a bit ... underwhelming.

225

Let us compare the presidencies of Reagan and Clinton. Under Reagan, the federal budget deficits were larger, the government grew faster, the economy grew slower, and the after-tax income of an average family (adjusted for inflation) grew less. And even though Reagan had the Iran-Contra affair, Clinton had the Lewinsky affair. Obviously, the blowjob tips the scale. Reagan wins the contest!

226

Conservatives distort President Reagan's record about as much as they distort the record of Jesus.

227

We should modify the duties of government regulators who neglect their responsibilities into ones that are better suited for them (i.e., regulating the conditions of their prison cells).

228

When I was only a child, my older brother, Tim, challenged me to my first game of *Monopoly*. He quickly exploited my inexperience —seizing every property and bankrupting me. But Tim's conquest was not big enough for him, so he grabbed the bank's pile of $50 bills and handed them over, declaring, "Your uncle died and left you some money!" Naturally, I accepted this modification to the game—though my newfound capital soon went to pay for rent, calling for further "inheritances" and rule changes. Before long, I was broke, *the bank was broke*, and Tim owned multiple hotels on each of the properties along with all of the game's cash. Thank you, Tim, for this painless lesson in free market capitalism.

229

While we are treating corporations like people, they are treating us like objects.

230

Christians should embrace men who love other men rather than men who *hate* other men.

231

Being religious means following rules—not acting morally.

232

When there is something that needs doing, just do it: by giving yourself a choice, you are merely facilitating procrastination.

233

We are blindly idolizing a new golden calf: the free market.

234

Compared to their Caucasian invaders, Native Americans were more peaceful—except for when they were more violent.

235

A note to creationists: *The Flintstones* was not actually based on a true story.

236

There is some truth at the core of every criticism.

237

Why are most journalists liberal? I maintain it is because they explore our country firsthand, seeing it all through the lens of reality, not political propaganda. By witnessing the results of conservative and liberal programs, journalists become singularly qualified to judge the effectiveness of party platforms. It is these insights that lead to verdicts against right-wing ideology.

238

With controversial legislative issues (such as deregulation) that receive bipartisan support, do not divvy up party responsibility equally without examining the vote. Even when members of both parties vote for a particular bill, one of them is usually the driving force behind its passage. This party—as champion of the cause —deserves all the credit (good or bad).

239

Asking a military leader if we should go to war is like asking a decathlete if we should go to the Olympics.

240

My experiences cause me to believe that women are generally more territorial than men are *in nonsexual situations*. In fact, just to avoid crossing any other lionesses, I am contemplating a move back to Mars.

241

Libertarian Rand Paul revealed the true objective of free market capitalists when he declared, "I'm not opposed to letting people come in and work and labor in our country. But I think what we should do is we shouldn't provide an easy route to citizenship." Put differently, slaveholders want to keep on exploiting slaves — while making it harder for them to win their freedom.

242

After the Civil War, we were unable to police the South, where forms of slavery thrived for nearly another century. *So why do we believe that we can do any better policing distant foreign countries?*

243

In his 1961 Farewell Address to the Nation, President Dwight Eisenhower gave a warning: "Only an alert and knowledgeable citizenry can compel the proper meshing of the huge industrial and military machinery of defense with our peaceful methods and goals so that security and liberty may prosper together." We are now spending roughly $1 trillion annually for defense-related purposes, about as much as all other countries in the world *combined*. Our perpetual war economy feeds an insatiable industry that will never consent to a diet. Put simply, we have disregarded Eisenhower's warning by ceding control of our armed forces to the military-industrial complex—thereby bankrupting our nation and condemning the world to constant warfare.

244

When responding to hostility, keep in mind that Jesus instructed us to turn the other cheek—not to *spread* the other cheek.

245

Mental illnesses should bear no more social stigma than physical illnesses do, for they all stem from the same type of sources.

246

Hormonal imbalances can generate mental illnesses—just ask any woman suffering from PMS (at your own risk).

247

Why do so many women insist that once a month all people and things coincidentally rebel against them?

248

Perhaps it would be easier for our leaders to wean us off oil if they used a catchy campaign phrase—such as "America's War on Oil."

249

We cannot hope for an energy policy much more sophisticated than "drill, baby, drill!" from politicians who draw up national policies as if their brains had been lobotomized *with a drill*.

250

There is something far more dangerous than a group of stupid people: a group of stupid people who think they are smart.

251

With societal issues, I am a liberal. With individual issues, I am a conservative. Although society should supply the means for all citizens to prosper, we remain individually responsible for what we make—or do not make—of our own lives.

252

Personal effort and responsibility will only take one as far in life as personal good fortune allows.

253

Of all forms of tyranny threatening Americans, one stands out as the most menacing: the tyranny of ignorant voters.

254

Allying with Israel while trying to befriend Arab countries was like bringing a fierce pit bull into the home of dog haters—hoping to win their friendship.

255

Israel has not protected our interests in the Middle East. We have protected *Israeli* interests.

256

To be religious is to be slothful, for belief is easy and reason is hard.

257

The strength of science comes from its brave self-assessments— and the strength of religion comes from its cowardly self-*deceptions*.

258

The bad news is that our students are doing poorly in science. The good news is that the worst of them are still doing far better than the clergy has done throughout history.

259

Even if reason eventually defeats belief, religion will never die. It will evolve—placing truth over dogma, meditation over ritual, spirituality over worship, and humanity *alongside* God.

260

If you search back far enough in history, *everyone* has ancestors that some hostile nation has conquered, brutalized, enslaved, or exterminated. Hence, any descendants who seek reparations for historical atrocities must first queue up with everyone else on earth.

261

The more the red states mangle our nation with their ill-advised political agendas, the more regularly I fantasize about the blue states having their own try at secession.

262

Labor unions provide essential checks and balances to managerial authority, but free market capitalists are brainwashing us into thinking that all unions are corrupt. We are to believe that business owners are the only decent citizens in the nation, and that those of us who dare to question them are anti-American Neanderthals destined for Hell. Of course, if we settle for the low wages, meager benefits, and wretched working conditions that management wishes to grant us—we might as well be in Hell.

263

If the death penalty does deter atrocious crimes, why are we not executing the CEOs of Halliburton, Goldman Sachs, Xe, and BP?

264

George W. Bush was the worst president in American history. I will submit no evidence to support my verdict: everywhere one looks, there is ample proof—if one chooses to see.

265

As the godfather of deregulation, "trickle-down" economics, and bloated military budgets, Ronald Reagan was the most destructive president in American history. The financial crash of 2008, the BP oil spill, the collapse of the middle class, the runaway federal debt, and the rampaging military-industrial complex are just a sampling of the current plights that he paved the way to. I wonder how far we must trudge down Reagan's path before enough voters realize that we took a ruinous turn in 1980.

266

Given that free market capitalists expect my government to clean up their "accidental" mishaps—I insist on giving Uncle Sam all the regulatory authority he needs to proactively prevent them.

267

In 1951, the democratically elected parliament of Iran selected Dr. Mohammed Mosaddeq for prime minister—and his global popularity led *Time* magazine to name him Man of the Year. His most notable act was to nationalize Iran's oil industry, taking it out of the grasp of BP. Mosaddeq said, "With the oil revenues we could meet our entire budget and combat poverty, disease, and backwardness among our people." After President Truman refused to intervene for BP, President Eisenhower authorized Operation Ajax: our CIA orchestrated a coup d'état in 1953 that knocked Mosaddeq and the elected government out of power, replacing them with a dictator, Shah Pahlavi. *Now connect the dots through the last six decades of Middle Eastern turmoil — and consider how much better off the world would have been with a democratic Iran instead of a richer oil company.*

268

There is only one aspect of communism that our government has never tolerated: community ownership of resources. To be our buddy, a Third World country must privatize its "commodities" (e.g., oil, coffee, water), permitting multinational corporations to acquire them at rock-bottom prices. If it nationalizes many of its resources to keep them in the hands of its people, we summarily assail it for being Marxist — and call it our enemy.

269

Campaign commercials are junk food for our brains. Sadly, they taste worse than horseshit and provide less nourishment than deep-fried Twinkies.

270

Army Regulation 525-13 clearly defines a terrorist group as "any element regardless of size or espoused cause, which repeatedly commits acts of violence or threatens violence in pursuit of its political, religious, or ideological objectives." Judging by this definition, our numerous military operations since World War II must appear hypocritical to many non-Americans — particularly after our Geneva Convention violations in Guantánamo Bay and Abu Ghraib. *In the eyes of the world, we too frequently look like the ultimate terrorist group.*

271

Even when facing a potentially unstoppable oil gusher that could become a significant extinction event, ignoramuses are still yelling, "Drill, baby, drill!" So just how hard must Mother Nature spank these greedy brats to get them to shut up and behave?

272

A capitalist's freedom fighter is most often a populist's terrorist.

273

I had been worried that before anybody could read this book, too many of my entries would no longer be timely. After giving this concern some deliberation, I realized it was unwarranted for two reasons: first, although the specifics of some events will fade into the past, the underlying issues are continually reborn; and second, when these events do fall victim to countrywide bouts of amnesia, my writings may help restore the memories.

274

From a victim's perspective, all armed aggression is terrorism.

275

God spoke to me today. He said, "Thou shalt not vote for any of those deceivers who schizophrenically claim that I told them to run."

276

The chase for loads of cash to purchase campaign advertising has transformed Washington into the world's largest brothel. But using public financing to cover these advertisement dependencies is not a practical remedy; *instead, we must break the need for ads*. With broadcast media, we should prohibit campaign commercials for national races—replacing them with infomercials that the major networks would freely air as a public service. To eliminate the need for print media ads, each candidate should write a book to set forth positions, which the government would distribute free of charge. A nonpartisan panel of experts would scrutinize all infomercials and books prior to public consumption to ensure the accuracy of facts and the viability of proposals. With these reasonable reforms, we can liberate candidates from their main campaign costs while serving voters meatier information to digest.

277

If two men are preparing to duel, and I give both of them a gun, most casual witnesses will believe that my relationships with the duelists are equal. This assumption would be wrong, however, if I had in fact armed one man with a handgun and the other with a squirt gun. *Thus, we must look closely when judging people by their campaign contributions*: if somebody gives cash to two competing politicians, never assume that the donor has the same friendship with each—for the real chum is the one awarded the deadliest gun.

278

The only people who should fear "gotcha journalism" are airheads (e.g., Sarah Palin), liars (e.g., Dick Cheney), and shammers who mask their true beliefs (e.g., all Tea Party candidates). It is worth noting that almost everyone who whines about gotcha journalism is a member of the GOP.

279

Third World citizens will probably give us little sympathy as we struggle with BP's oil spill—and that would make us even. For years, unrestrained multinational corporations have habitually poisoned developing countries. So how much sympathy did we give their citizens after our free market capitalists destroyed their lands? Only now will these violated people win a bit of justice—though it will merely be "poetic" in nature.

280

Rush Limbaugh won the award for the most crackbrained allegation of 2010 by saying, "There's no question that payback is what this [President Obama's] administration is all about, presiding over the decline of the United States of America, and doing so happily." Rush then ravingly contended that the president wants Americans to be unemployed and to lose all hope so that they can learn what it was like ("in Obama's view") for black people over the last 230 years. The scariest aspect of this insane claim is that hordes of "dittoheads" swallowed each of these race-baiting words with relish.

281

When weighing the merits of personal bankruptcy, view it through a capitalist's green-tinted glasses: it is not the dishonorable surrender of a loser; rather, it is a prudent business strategy.

282

Capitalism, socialism, and communism are all viable economic systems—until an unscrupulous party undermines them to seize tyrannical power (i.e., Nazi-like malevolence can emerge from *any* environment).

283

If bigmouths drown out your words every time you try to exercise your freedom of speech, *you do not have freedom of speech*.

284

Radio and television are our main forums for political dialogue. However, due to the high costs of airtime, our dialogue is one-sided: only wealthy citizens have regularly aired voices. This imbalance seriously threatens our democracy, for tyranny gains a foothold when many of us do not have the same freedom of speech. To guarantee that everyone can similarly participate in our political forums, we must expand free public access to radio and television broadcast facilities.

285

If 90% of talk radio was liberal rather than conservative, would Limbaugh or Beck then see the jeopardy to our public discourse? (They might, but it probably would not bother them too much as long as there was no jeopardy to their own wallets.)

286

The wellbeing of our democracy is of far greater import than the *privilege* of radio corporations to monopolize our limited public frequencies.

287

There is no doubt that Dr. Joseph Goebbels would have sided with those who oppose restoring the Fairness Doctrine. After all, it would obstruct current efforts to flood our airwaves with propaganda.

288

If we had handled our slavery problems entirely by deporting token Africans—*instead of by banning slaveholding*—businesses would still exploit slaves today. So why are we using this lame approach to halt the exploitation of undocumented immigrant laborers?

289

Watching BP clean up the oil spill is like watching housekeepers tidy up a filthy home by sweeping everything under the carpets.

290

The surest way for Republicans to prove their assertion that our government was broken was for them to break it. So they did.

291

Voting for a third-party presidential candidate who has no real chance of winning is as pointless as joining protesters that are flipping the bird at a passing windstorm: it will go by without altering course—with no recollection of your party's positions or demands.

292

Democrats and Republicans both have large numbers of low-income supporters: generally, the urban poor lean Democratic while the rural poor lean Republican. Each party must peddle the benefits of its platform to preserve and expand its share of poor voters. When talking about the economy, Democrats can exhibit their many social programs, which are not tough to sell. Republicans, on the other hand, have nothing better to offer than "trickle-down" tax cuts for the aristocracy; hence, to make their crucial sale to the poor, they become lying hucksters pitching a product that is inappropriate for their targeted buyers. *Moreover, since it is easier to play this "confidence trick" on the unschooled, the GOP is pursuing a decades-long strategy to dismantle our educational system.* Ignorance is the lube of the Republican machine.

293

To keep people ignorant of their ignorance, award unmerited diplomas.

294

The GOP exploits deficient English skills with euphemisms (e.g., civilian deaths are acceptable when called "collateral damage" and torture is appropriate when called "enhanced interrogation").

295

To teach children art, we first have them do fun activities like finger painting. Only after a few years of hooking them on such assignments do we begin to introduce art theory. This is how we should teach English—creativity long before grammar.

296

The fate of the GOP agenda hinges on the wisdom of Edmund Burke: "Those who don't know history are destined to repeat it." It is by warping our memory of history that the GOP can keep reselling the same harmful policies to lower- and middle-class voters. If too many of us were to dig too deeply into the past 30 years—recalling how the GOP has repeatedly enriched the wealthy at our expense—the party would need to abandon its agenda or perish.

297

History should be a popular academic subject: most of us love stories—and by sharing historical ones, we learn from the past. Nevertheless, too few teachers fully use the storytelling process when exposing their students to history. Schools prefer the rote memorization of names and dates, which are more readily tested and graded. Unfortunately, after our uninterested students have regurgitated this hollow data, it swiftly fades from memory. *If we sincerely want to gain wisdom from the successes and failures of the past, we must focus more on stories and less on minutiae.*

298

Republican efforts to control the rabble have made it far easier for poor citizens to go to prison—and far harder for them to go to universities. This strengthens the GOP's "tough on crime" image while purging probable opposition voters (i.e., lower-class university graduates most often vote Democratic, but convicts and many ex-convicts do not get to vote at all).

299

Although zero-tolerance policies violate our rights to *due process of law* and *no cruel and unusual punishment,* they also please our tyrants and simpletons. So what does the widespread reliance on zero tolerance in schools tell us about our educators? And what do such policies teach our children about justice?

300

By being thrifty with universities and their students, we do not make them leaner; we make them anemic. Universities are begging for resources and cutting corners on educational services, while students are spending far more of their limited time working instead of learning. One does not need a degree to comprehend that this is an idiotic misuse of brainpower.

301

It is much easier to win someone's support for a military action when that person is clueless concerning where the target country lies on a map or what the "enemy" is like. In other words, with our failure to learn elementary geography and sociology, we have given our leaders a free hand to attack any country.

302

Democracy is a complex machine, and our citizenry is responsible for its upkeep. Since the care of any complex machine calls for education to minimize breakage, we have civics classes to teach the workings of government. But despite the vital role these classes play in preserving a healthy democracy, schools—mainly poor ones—are quietly marginalizing and eliminating them. The societal price for this slashing of civics is high: with little understanding of government and their place in it, young persons are less likely to participate and vote—while those who do are more likely to fall victim to manipulative politicians. This is "coincidently" an optimal outcome for the GOP—particularly for the way it affects impoverished citizens.

303

Beyond teaching us about the universe, science classes build our reasoning skills. Without these, beliefs guide us—or *mis*guide us. And that explains the GOP's war on science: our children's beliefs in things like Santa please us—just as our silly, feel-good beliefs in things like free markets, supply-side economics, stable climates, and American exceptionalism please the GOP.

304

In response to a slave rebellion in 1831, several states enacted laws to ban the teaching of all black people. In 2008, Congress passed the Post-9/11 Veterans Educational Assistance Act *without the backing of many Republicans who argued that it would lead to more troops refusing to re-enlist.* These two events show that our aristocracy has always recognized the need to control access to education when subjugating the masses.

305

By sabotaging our educational system—thereby disempowering our citizens—corporations could create an army of wage slaves. Of course, to implement such a vile plan, these moneygrubbers would need accomplices—such as a political party of capitalist toadies....

306

If you do not learn your sums in school, the GOP will bamboozle you with its brand of creative math (e.g., claiming that we can cut tax revenues collected from millionaires without increasing our budget deficits).

307

With shrinking job opportunities and pay—and skyrocketing student debt—university graduates have become our modern day indentured servants.

308

Imagine a country that has repealed or severely weakened most of its laws. In this anarchic environment, mobs seize great wealth and power. The police, already understaffed, are paid off—and puppet judges limit sentences to relatively minor fines. As the parasitic mobs increasingly prosper, the people become ever more deprived. *Now substitute the words "laws," "mobs," and "police" with "regulations," "banks," and "regulators"—and reassess this fantastic reality.*

309

Third-party presidential candidates serve little purpose besides playing spoilers, *unless they hold the centrist position between the*

Republican and Democratic nominees. A "long shot" who fails to seize this position will merely split the votes from one side of the political spectrum, much to the delight of the lone party at the other end. By taking the center, the long shot can play the two major party candidates against each other while siphoning off voters from both.

310

Police officers have gained the unconstitutional power to arrest anybody at any time for any reason. Remarkably vague disorderly conduct laws grant them sweeping authority to detain us for authentic, indefinite, or *potential* disturbances.   Although this "catch-all" charge can create long-lasting difficulties in one's life, police still issue citations for it as if they were giving out baseball cards. This is a cunning way to control the rabble—but alarmingly, *you and I are that rabble*.

311

I understand the frustration and rage that can drive some police officers to beat known criminals. In fact, I shamefully confess that in a stressful enough situation, with a big enough trigger, I would assault a scumbag. Because of this trait, I am unqualified to serve. *Now we just need current and would-be officers to be equally honest.*

312

Not every liar is a thief—but every thief is a liar.

313

For-profit colleges are the payday lenders of our post-secondary educational system: they exploit the needy by indebting them for overhyped, overpriced services.

314

We should send a human to Mars so that we can offer our children another Neil Armstrong instead of another Tiger Woods.

315

When liberals criticize our government, conservatives label them anti-American communists who should leave the country—but when Tea Partiers criticize our government, conservatives give them praise, labeling them pro-American patriots who should run for office.

316

The same unethical breed of "scientists" who sold their souls to Big Tobacco—muddying the facts on the dangers of smoking—now dupe us for Big Oil, muddying the facts on the dangers of global warming. This time, their noxious deceits will afflict the entire planet. These betrayers must be getting loads of silver.

317

Who stands to earn more wealth by winning over the public in the global warming debate—university nerds or Big Oil nerds?

318

Contrary to what fear mongers want us to believe, terrorists are typically brainless. They are much like our blue-collar crooks, dumb and drugged. The shoe, underwear, and Times Square bombers have little in common with the villains from 24.

319

When Eric Cartman grows up, he will be the next Glenn Beck.

320

Divorce—not same-sex marriage—presents the gravest threat to conventional marriage. Maybe we should outlaw divorce.

321

Religions often oppose same-sex marriages on the grounds that homosexual couples cannot procreate. How would we react if the same argument led religions to ban all marriages of infertile *hetero*sexuals? Also, would we permit the state to follow suit?

322

Many people are homophobic simply because any imagery of gay sex disgusts them. But I have a newsflash for each of these bigots: *imagery of you having sex disgusts a majority of Americans.* Are you ready for us to vote on *your* sexual rights?

323

Until 1967, many states banned interracial marriages. One judge ruled that "Almighty God created the races white, black, yellow, malay and red, and he placed them on separate continents. And but for the interference with his arrangement there would be no cause for such marriages. The fact that he separated the races shows that he did not intend for the races to mix." This insane reasoning echoes now in the voices that argue to keep the ban on same-sex marriages. If President Obama will not condemn *this* discrimination, perhaps it would be proper for the government to prohibit his daughters from marrying outside their own race.

324

Even if we legalize same-sex marriages, a church is still free to decide which couples it will wed—*and which it will keep persecuting.*

325

By comparing each class's share of national after-tax income, we see that the gap between *the richest 1%* and *the lower and middle classes* is now greater than at any period since before the Great Depression. Despite this, the GOP keeps crusading for further tax breaks for our economic victors. I submit that nothing short of a *master-slave gap* will ever satisfy it.

326

Republican politicians are all Eddie Haskell clones, indignantly calling out the Democratic Party for the misdeeds that they are themselves guilty of routinely committing.

327

The wars in Vietnam, Afghanistan, and Iraq share one significant similarity: our leaders utilized *identical* lies and propaganda.

328

When Americans believe a profession is harmful to the country (e.g., bookmaking, prostitution, drug dealing), they obstinately outlaw it. So until we are certain that oil companies can and will do offshore drilling without endangering our environment, *it should be banned.* Any laid-off oil riggers can be rehired to clean up the BP spill and to develop green energy supplies. At this time, we need offshore oil traffickers as much as we need drug traffickers.

329

There is a direct relationship between how loudly one makes an argument and the impotency of that argument. Accordingly, it is nearly impossible to get a word in edgewise when debating Tea Partiers or their cousins.

330

A hotel receives its revenues from occupants. To maximize its revenues, it must maximize occupancy. Privatized prisons operate in a similar way. Of course, *hotel* lobbyists cannot get politicians to enact laws to lock nonviolent citizens into vacant rooms for prolonged stays. We lead the world in incarceration population, which has more than quadrupled since 1980—to the satisfaction of prison owners.

331

Letting Wall Street bosses fix our financial system is as unwise as letting mafia bosses fix our criminal justice system. We all know how such crooks always try to "fix" things.

332

Tea Partiers are not fighting for the rights of ordinary people, but for the rights of their corporate puppet masters.

333

I embrace all my prior experiences, good *and* bad, for without every one of them, I would not be who I am right now.

334

We should never blame victims—but some of them can share a bit of the responsibility.

335

Even if we cut federal spending down to nothing, Tea Partiers will keep hacking at it—for in their collective insanity, it is an undying demon from Hell.

336

In the real world, the bedrock of free market capitalism is not competition, but rather collusion and monopolization.

337

If a country implemented economic sanctions against *us*, we would universally condemn its action as an ignoble act of war.

338

For all nations, public programs and services are like fruits and vegetables: we can safely cut some of them out of our diet—but if we cut out too many, we *will* get sick.

339

Our aristocrats ferment the world's most expensive "whines."

340

President Obama has the same likelihood of appeasing right-wingers as a bird has of appeasing cats. Since nothing besides resignation will placate his antagonists, every concession is a pointless sacrifice that wounds our country and tarnishes his record. *When someone is determined to crucify you, do not furnish the nails.*

341

America treats wars like sporting events. "Winning" is all that matters: death, destruction, and torment are simply part of the game. Even worse, we are poor sports, never caring how we play —as long as we prevail. This insane drive to win at all costs is the strongest political obstacle that keeps us from escaping our mess in Afghanistan. *We must stop crippling our "opponents" and ourselves by finding less dangerous ways to sate our hunger for flag-waving triumph.*

342

I support public ownership and management of all essential resources (e.g., water, fuel, electricity) and services (e.g., national defense, healthcare, education). Otherwise, for all *non*essentials, I support private ownership with regulated markets. This mix of socialism and capitalism plays to their strengths while reducing exposure to their flaws.

343

If you cannot believe what scientists say regarding the workings of evolution, perhaps first-hand confirmation from a best friend will help: go talk with your dog about its family tree.

344

I praise WikiLeaks for carrying out the societal duties that our mainstream media can no longer discharge due to the muzzles of its corporate masters.

345

The truths that steer us out of wars will always shed less blood than the lies that steer us *into* wars.

346

In general, nonprofit organizations are equivalent to *for*-profit organizations, with one noteworthy difference: nonprofits have no investors to set their agendas, so they are free to pursue goals other than net-income maximization. Instead of merely offering lip service to philanthropy via their mission statements, they can genuinely labor to improve our world. Nonetheless, since they lack an impulsion to generate wealth, capitalists have taught us to view nonprofits as second-class outfits.

347

Owing to my severe disability, inadequate income, and nonexistent wealth, Medicaid pays for my personal care attendants—without whom I could not live. Though I have interviewed about a thousand applicants for this work, only an infinitesimal fraction of them leaned to the right (yes, I do always ask). Put differently, despite the reasonable pay for this job, conservatives have little interest in it. Moreover, they participate even less in social services that are *un*paid. So when these individuals push to replace publicly funded programs with volunteerism, we should disregard the scheme—*for it springs from hustlers who are too greedy to ever work for free.*

348

Capitalists have another name for volunteers: suckers.

349

The phrase "I can't wait for tomorrow" is the deadliest killer of today. *Do not so carelessly dispose of the present.*

350

Apple has the most loyal customers that marketing can buy. Even though its competitors' products normally have superior features for the price, Apple remains the crème de la crème. *And it is—as it likes to remind us—so much nicer than that "evil" Microsoft.* If you disagree, do not worry: Apple will keep overcharging dupes so that it can use its inflated income to brainwash you too, in time.

351

A journalist who lacks skills in analysis and debate is unfit to report on anything more contentious than grade school sports.

352

We did not invade Iraq to grab its black gold for ourselves. We invaded Iraq to grab its black gold for *Big Oil*.

353

We would all find the will to moderate our social inequities if the rich and poor could walk in each other's universe for a day.

354

After convincing us to buy unsafe products, manufacturers feign innocence, insisting that they are just selling what consumers are demanding.

355

Politically correct language is an essential survival mechanism for bigots: it allows them to blend safely into society as they harass their prey.

356

Immediately after Barack Obama won the presidency, the DNC should have denounced Fox News for being a GOP propaganda machine while calling on Democrats to boycott the station by declining requests to be on air. Fox is free to perpetuate its "fair and balanced" farce, but its adversaries should not legitimize its tilted news by actively participating. (Incidentally, it is still not too late to put this plan into action.)

357

If we refuse to pay off our ecological debts, Mother Nature will someday break a lot more than our legs.

358

The inhumanities of the Nazis did not sprout from socialism, but rather from fascism—an ideology rooted in *far-right* politics.

359

The national debt that we are passing on to our heirs stems from our unwillingness to pay the full price for our public services. Similarly, with our consumption of underpriced commodities, we are bequeathing incalculable ecological debts. America has evolved into a nation of freeloaders.

360

An uncommon exception never invalidates a generality—for in our multifaceted world, there are exceptions to everything.

361

Nice people too often call for tolerance in order to avoid giving criticism; conversely, nasty people too often call for tolerance in order to avoid *receiving* criticism.

362

Since Glenn Beck is fervently against social justice, he must be for social *in*justice. His idolaters appear to have no awareness of this logical conclusion—and it is their blindness that most alarms me. Beck is demonstrating how a fascist can warp and win the public heart.

363

The "rational" self-interest of an ordinary adult seldom matures beyond the juvenile desire for an unending diet of ice cream and cake. This explains why free market capitalism quickly sickens.

364

Through my entire life, I have used a wheelchair—and strangers have stared. Their curiosity and ensuing judgments do not upset me, however, for I have learned to shut them out of my mind. By so doing, I disempower their naive appraisals. I know what I am worth, and no stranger will sway my estimate. This is my secret to maintaining a healthy self-esteem.

365

The Gulf States twice voted unanimously for George Bush and Dick Cheney—the sworn champions of deregulation and Big Oil. I guess the BP oil spill vividly confirms that "whatsoever a man soweth, that shall he also reap." Unfortunately, these states will now force all taxpayers to partake of their fool's harvest.

366

Capitalism is a self-destructive system, for its primary engine is competition, which every capitalist sets out to destroy.

367

Even if someone discovered the Fountain of Youth, it would do us little good. First, pharmaceutical chemists would synthesize an impotent—yet patentable—imitation. Then, Big Pharma lobbyists would convince the Drug Enforcement Administration to criminalize the "unsafe" and "addictive" spring waters. Some people would still score the real stuff: the wealthy ones would be young again and free, whereas all others would be young again and jailed. The rest of us, meanwhile, would go bankrupt buying the chemical knockoff, enriching our "legitimate" drug barons as we poison ourselves, dose by dose.

368

Pharmaceuticals feed us their food additives (e.g., olestra and aspartame), ruining our health—and then feed us their drugs in an effort to undo the damage. This is Big Pharma's cycle of life.

369

In July 2010—only 21 months after President Bush bulldozed the bank bailout through Congress—the Pew Research Center found that only 34% of those polled knew that Bush had signed the bill into law, while 47% blamed President Obama. The uninformed, the misinformed, and the amnesiacs have again granted amnesty to the GOP.

370

Religions enable us to see ourselves as essential, eternal—as the center of a universe that caters just to us. In essence, we come to see ourselves as gods. *This arrogance is the ultimate blasphemy.*

371

To maximize your power, identify your biggest "weakness" and use it to your advantage (e.g., a disability can open doors that are not generally accessible).

372

We are no longer cave dwellers, so let us at last recognize that true power now derives from a large brain—not a large club.

373

After ruthlessly minimizing your material wants, reward yourself by acquiring those that remain.

374

In 1970, Nixon political strategist Kevin Phillips explained the GOP's Southern Strategy: "The more Negroes who register as Democrats in the South, the sooner the Negrophobe whites will quit the Democrats and become Republicans. That's where the votes are." Hence, the Republican heirs of Abraham Lincoln have sold out the people he emancipated—just to pick up the votes of racists.

375

To win assistance from programs with limited resources, people compete against one another in contests to establish who is the neediest. The cost of this *competing victimization* is steep: when role-playing the victim, one often becomes that victim. *As you seek a hand to help you up, try not to tumble further down.*

376

Corporate America is a ventriloquist, using the Tea Party as its dummy: with *every* policy concern (e.g., social spending, taxes, regulations), the Tea Party *always* mouths the corporate positions; however, under closer scrutiny, we can see corporate America's lips moving as it subtly manipulates the dummy's actions.

377

If federal regulations are so horribly improper, as Tea Partiers regularly preach, why are they not fighting to rip up the mother of all regulatory documents—the United States Constitution.

378

Our mainstream media fawns over the Tea Party for a very good reason: they share the same daddy. Corporate America.

379

Too many Americans are too busy or too lazy to safeguard our democracy—and that is just the way our aristocrats want it to be.

380

From the Revolutionary War through World War II, black soldiers served within segregated units. Opponents of integration argued that many white soldiers would never live and fight beside black ones, that morale would suffer, and that the military should not be a tool for social experimentation. Now the newest generation of bigots is regurgitating the same idiocies to prevent the open integration of gay soldiers. *Let us again assure Chicken Little and his fretful animal friends that the sky is not falling.*

381

In the real world of business, free market capitalists magically become impure: although they keep believing that taxation and regulations are sinful, government subsidies and protectionism soon entice them all. This universal infidelity to the holy creed of *laissez-faire* economics is a well-kept, dirty secret.

382

Sarah Palin, Dr. Laura Schlessinger, and other right-wing media pundits should someday take a moment to read the 45 words of the First Amendment: it does not entitle anyone to have a talk show blessed with adoring fans, nor does it shelter media celebrities from the criticisms of those who choose to exercise their own freedom of speech. (Also, its text does not constrain our right to patronize—or boycott—the sponsors of *any* show.)

383

The easiness of a path bears little on its appropriateness.

384

About 30% of Americans are diehard Republicans. These people will endorse *anything* that features the GOP label. If Beelzebub became president and tortured all of us, I am certain he would still get a 30% approval rating—as long as he wore a GOP hat.

385

Bloomberg Businessweek has disclosed that News Corp., the parent company of Fox News, gave $1 million to the Republican Governors Association. This huge bankrolling of the GOP dispels the final wispy illusions of Fox News being "fair and balanced." From now on, to reflect its actual role as the media arm of the GOP, I will refer to this channel as Fox *Propaganda*.

386

The best "Christian" candidate for a public office is the one who is faking it.

387

The controversy over the building of an Islamic community center and mosque near Ground Zero still rages, and America has already stumbled halfway down the slippery slope leading to restrictions on the free exercise of religion. Across our nation, people are blocking the construction of mosques, *proving that denomination, not location, is the real issue angering most protestors*. We gave up too many rights with past knee-jerk reactions to 9/11 (e.g., the Patriot Act), so let us not award the terrorists another victory by restraining *anybody's* religious freedom.

388

The bones of 20,000 African slaves lie buried in the Ground Zero area. Because many mosque protesters insist that America has always been a Christian land, I believe that we must hold Christianity responsible for the unholy crimes that led to these deaths. Of course, this would then force us to bar Christians from erecting new *churches* upon this *twice*-hallowed ground.

389

Our society's reluctance to differentiate love from sex leads many young adults into wrongly believing that they are madly in love with their sex partners. Pregnancies and divorces soon follow.

390

Concerning the mosque near Ground Zero, Fox *Propaganda* vilified, by association, the project's organizer, Imam Feisal Abdul Rauf: "The Kingdom Foundation, which has been a funder of Imam Rauf in the past ... is this Saudi organization headed up by the guy who tried to give Rudy Giuliani $10 million after 9/11 that was sent back. He funds radical madrasahs all over the world." So, who is this *unnamed* financier of evil? He is Saudi prince Al-Waleed bin Talal, the largest individual investor (after the Murdochs) in the parent corporation of Fox. *Rupert is truly keeping some "shady" company.*

391

In a fair world, we would send Rupert Murdoch and Roger Ailes to prison for laundering counterfeit news at Fox *Propaganda*.

392

Monsanto is successfully pressuring farmers around the world to buy its genetically engineered seeds, which will supposedly produce higher yields. Since farmers cannot save the seeds from one crop to plant another (as they do with standard seeds), they must regularly pay for replacements. Monsanto is little more than an exploitative drug dealer that is turning global farmers into crack addicts.

393

I used to be a steadfast Republican, but I now see through their tricks and lies. If I can do it, you can do it!

394

In 1992, RNC Chairman Rich Bond admitted that trashing the media for being "liberal" was just a right-wing scheme: "If you watch any great coach, what they try to do is 'work the refs.' Maybe the ref will cut you a little slack next time." Now, with Fox *Propaganda* in the game, the GOP *owns* a bunch of the "refs."

395

Rupert Murdoch, the founder of Fox *Propaganda*, asserted that his channel has "given room to both sides, whereas only one side had it before." There lies the root of your deceits, Mr. Murdoch: legitimate news has only one side—*the truth*. By intentionally reporting *and promoting* other "sides," you are propagandizing.

396

In *The Wealth of Nations*, Adam Smith—an early theoretician of free markets—warned us that a laborer "generally becomes as stupid and ignorant as it is possible for a human creature to become."

He added that "this is the state into which the labouring poor, that is, the great body of the people, must necessarily fall, unless government takes some pains to prevent it." This clearly sounds like Smith was calling for *socialistic* intervention.

397

Few persons would ever choose to associate with someone who was vindictive, demanding, impulsive, hypocritical, judgmental, unforgiving, prejudiced, interfering, brooding, jealous, wrathful, violent, unfair, and needy. So why does half the world worship God (aka Allah and Yahweh)? With him as our top role model, it should be no surprise that humanity is terribly dysfunctional.

398

If President Obama ever kissed Saudi Crown Prince Abdullah and strolled with him, hand in hand, through a flower garden— *just as President George W. Bush did in 2005*—every right-wing media figure would instantaneously suffer brain hemorrhaging. Then, after recovering, they would argue even more insanely for impeachment.

399

Our cultural obsession with romantic fictions that involve vampires —*undead princes of soulless evil*—arises from the inability of many persons (particularly young women) to distinguish love from lust in their partners.

400

By neglecting to confront wrongdoings, we passively relabel them as proper deeds. Democratic leaders should have considered this truism before electing to forgo investigations into the unethical activities of the George W. Bush administration.

401

An informed vote equals an *un*informed or *mis*informed vote: this is the primary defect inherent to all democracies.

402

The newest defense for racists is to counterattack their victims by crying out, "Stop playing the race card." This is absurd: it is like having a trial where the accused chastises the victim for playing the "crime" card.

403

Even though the Declaration of Independence states, "All men are created equal," after we are born, *in*equality becomes the norm.

404

In an afterlife, God would never need Hell: upon our deaths, he could simply grant us complete knowledge of our misdeeds and their consequences, along with fully functioning consciences — and the worst persons would create their own private hells.

405

Single-issue liberals are selfish hypocrites.

406

Glenn Beck advised, "If you have a priest that is pushing social justice, go find another parish." But he got it backwards: you should look elsewhere if your priest *is not* pushing social justice. Such priests are heretics, walking contrary to the unambiguous path of Jesus.

407

The many evangelistic moles in our military pose a more insidious threat to our democracy than does an army of Islamic terrorists.

408

A Muslim who fails to condemn Islamic terrorist groups is better than a Christian who refuses to even recognize the existence of Christian terrorist groups within America (e.g., the Hutaree, the Ku Klux Klan, the Aryan Nations, Christian Patriots, the Army of God)—and around the world (e.g., Christian Identity groups).

409

Other objects in our country are hurtful besides the mosque by Ground Zero. For example, Confederate flags revolt my African wife and me: whenever we see one, it reminds us of the bigots that still yearn to dominate those who are different. Ironically, many of the proud "Stars and Bars" wavers are the ones most aggressively protesting the building of this mosque.

410

While scientists are diligently filling the gaps in our knowledge with research, theologians are still doing nothing more than filling these ever-disappearing gaps with God.

411

I support tort reform. Specifically, we must make it harder for corporations to abuse our court system. We should not tolerate their mobs of lawyers bullying individuals and small businesses. Also, by restricting the power of corporations to delay trials, to pursue frivolous appeals, and to challenge open-and-shut cases, we can cut legal costs. But this is all a dream: as Daniel Fisher explained in *Forbes*, tort reform is purely a "catchall phrase for legislative measures designed to make it harder for individuals to sue businesses," and "has long been a pet project of Republicans."

412

In 2005, when President Bush tried to privatize Social Security, he alarmed citizens by stating, "There is no 'trust fund'—just IOUs." He failed to explain that the IOUs are *government bonds*, backed by the full faith and credit of the U.S. Treasury. These Social Security *investments* are as good as cash. I suspect that after someone drew a crayon picture to dumb down all of this for Dubya, he merely took the simplification a bit too literally.

413

James Madison—the "Father of the Constitution" and our fourth president—successfully argued at the Constitutional Convention that our government must be designed "to protect the minority of the opulent against the majority." So our wealthy founders stacked the deck in the opulent's favor from the very beginning, although it is always the *non*-opulent majority that really needs protection.

414

The wealthy have no real reason to fear us—as long as they do not earn our wrath through *excessive* exploitation.

415

Albert Einstein said that insanity is "doing the same thing over and over again and expecting different results." Judging by his definition, all the voters who plan to again cast ballots for GOP candidates in the 2010 congressional elections are in urgent need of immediate psychiatric care.

416

Our country is sexually repressed and desensitized to violence—a condition continually exacerbated by the film rating system of the Motion Picture Association of America (MPAA). To grasp the problem, examine two movies from 1995: *Seven*, a story with unforgettably gruesome murders; and *Showgirls*, a story with sex and nudity. Though the former got an R rating while the latter got an NC-17, just the synopsis of *Seven* can turn one's stomach. The only thing more disturbing than watching its graphic cruelty is the knowledge that the MPAA and other viewers found the flashing of naked breasts to be even worse.

417

Right-wing pundits say that President Obama hates America—so I say that George W. Bush insanely loathes the whole cosmos and is a poopy-face booger eater. *Just grow up already!*

418

Scientists theorize that our universe began as a point with zero volume and infinite density—a singularity that held all matter and energy, ungoverned by our laws of physics. Inexplicably, it exploded, creating space, time, and in due course, everything we know today. This explains what my god was, what my god did, and how we evolved out of this universal entity. I can perceive god within every person, creature, and object.

419

"Competition is a sin, therefore you must destroy it," said John D. Rockefeller, America's first billionaire. This dictum became the first commandment in the holy bible of capitalism. And with the blessings of our bribed government, corporate America has nearly vanquished this sin.

420

Instead of detaining individuals for "reasonable suspicion," too many police officers base their detentions on the unofficial legal standard of "reasonable pretext."

421

If we allow Monsanto to genetically modify our world's food with scarcely any testing or oversight, we are not permitting the company to play god. Rather, we are permitting it *to be* god.

422

America loves to have "friendly" dictatorships, not democracies, running Third World nations: a firm leader can ensure a setting conducive to the long-term corporate exploitation of resources— while an authentic democracy is fickle and more likely to pursue agendas contrary to those of big business.

423

A number of our celebrated Third World "democracies" are no more democratic than was Florida in 2000 or Ohio in 2004.

424

I do not know if anabolic steroids are dangerous—but I do know we cannot trust the assessment of a government that continues to demonize marijuana.

425

The more often a person labels others as sexists or racists, the more often that person should examine a mirror to confirm that a bigot is not staring back.

426

Legal does not mean safe—nor does *il*legal mean *un*safe.

427

Arizona's immigration act, SB 1070, enables people to sue public officials and agencies that fail to enforce national immigration laws to the full extent permitted by the federal government. It is unfortunate that legislators will never allow us to sue those who refuse to fully enforce laws covering *white-collar crimes.*

428

In a southern border state like Arizona, asking police officers to detain undocumented immigrants *without particularly targeting nonwhite races* (i.e., racially profiling) is akin to asking big-game hunters to cage rabid Ursidae without particularly targeting bears. It is disingenuous to suggest that this is a doable assignment.

429

A society based on Ayn Rand's teachings can work out for the selfish only as long as there is an abundance of the self*less.*

430

For every constitutional right that the Tea Party sticks up for, it stabs two others in the back.

431

With only two changes, we can make Social Security permanently solvent: first, eliminate benefits for the wealthy because they have no need and they have already milked society's wallet enough; and second, assess FICA taxes on 100% of their earnings so that they can contribute to the "pensions" of every worker they have exploited to obtain their fortunes.

432

Racism is less about hatred and more about disrespect.

433

What some persons label "socialism," others label "an attempt to save democracy."

434

Whenever Americans protest any of our wars, the GOP publicly reprimands the activists for emboldening the enemy. But when the Dove World Outreach Center (a trivial Christian fundamentalist cult) threatened to burn Qur'ans, a crowbar could not pry apart Republican lips, even though General Petraeus warned us that the images of such a burning "would undoubtedly be used by extremists in Afghanistan—and around the world—to inflame public opinion and incite violence." Combine this situation with the GOP stoking of anger against the "Ground Zero" mosque, and a telling portrait emerges of the typical Republican official: he cares far less about our soldiers than his rhetoric professes; he ignites bigotry when it helps him politically; and he defends the First Amendment rights of only like-minded people.

435

The Patriot Act defines one class of domestic terrorism as "acts dangerous to human life that are a violation of the criminal laws" and that "appear to be intended to intimidate or coerce a civilian population." Under this broad definition, the torching of Qur'ans in public without a burn permit is terrorism. Though Pastor Terry Jones got away with it, a "nobody" might not.

436

Either "all men" are sluttish pigs that will screw anything with two legs—or they are shallow boars that will screw only women with large breasts. Both generalities cannot be valid. To be fair, female chauvinists should pick just one of these sexist condemnations to dogmatize.

437

Nostalgia is the longing for a past that probably never even existed.

438

Those who fight for states' rights are often fighting for tyranny. They seek to replace the vast representative will of our nation with the smaller representative wills of states—*which politicians can more readily manipulate and control*. These petty leaders can then define our rights while they rule over their own miniature countries.

439

Beyond geographic and climatic variations, there are no major differences between the states: people are people wherever they live, having similar rights and needs (e.g., social safety nets, healthcare, education). Nevertheless, we let the states dictate our rights and needs as they see fit. This guarantees that many Americans will find themselves shortchanged and—because of the residency requirements that must be met to receive services when moving to a new state—shackled behind a border.

440

For each state that protects the rights of its citizens, another does not, multiplying our need for activists—*who are then divided and conquered along state lines*.

441

By reciprocating Islamic fundamentalist deviltries with Christian fundamentalist deviltries—and vice versa—unholy crusades will continue to rage throughout the ages.

442

People who openly carry guns violate my right to be free from intimidation: given that I cannot tell if they are "terrorists" or not, I must assume the worst and move to safety, surrendering *my* public liberties.

443

Today is 9/11. The media is again pummeling us with images from nine years ago, reawakening all of our fears from the event. As long as our country keeps harboring these paralytic feelings, it will never *rationally* examine the falsehoods of the attacks. In other words, at the current time, *we can't handle the truth*.

444

The more thoroughly we cut politicians and their minions out of the picture, the better our democracy will function. We common folk are quite capable of discovering facts and weighing them to formulate solutions—if we can seize an opportunity. Democracy draws its strength from networking the minds of the multitudes, not merely the privileged few.

445

In August 2010, a *Time* magazine survey revealed that 24% of Americans believe President Obama is a Muslim. The breadth of this ignorance is unsettling—but the fervor over this *non*issue is even worse.

446

America's economy would be much more stable if Wall Street handled stocks as if they were shares of corporate ownership — as opposed to baseball trading cards.

447

I have a question for those who argue that public schools should teach creationism and other beliefs from the Bible: what do you prefer *madrasahs* to teach children, evolution and other scientific subjects—*or beliefs from the Qur'an?*

448

Modern medicine is enabling people with severe genetic disorders to survive and reproduce. This will weaken our gene pool, but— of more import to the long-term wellbeing of humanity—it will also strengthen our pools of compassion and understanding.

449

In 2007, Tea Party sweetheart Christine O'Donnell maintained that scientists were "cross-breeding humans and animals and coming up with mice with fully functioning human brains." Right-wing nuts need to stop learning their science from *Dexter's Laboratory.*

450

It has become taboo for us to discuss politics with most people, and it is choking democracy. Without vigorous public discourse, we become lost sheep. As such, every wannabe tyrant can herd us onto treacherous lands without a bleat of protest. If we want to keep power within our hands, *we must stop censoring ourselves and courageously debate* all *issues.*

451

Businesses are not an entitlement program for owners: they have no more right to turn a profit than they do a loss.

452

If you make more in a year than what we pay the President of the United States, you are, by any sensible definition, *filthy* rich.

453

People can become filthy rich only through inheritance, luck, or fraud. Although none of these avenues should merit a person any respect or the lower tax rates of honest workers, we keep giving both. We do this primarily because we have fallen for a capitalist lie: specifically, *that our hard work can make us just as wealthy*.

454

Christine O'Donnell argued that evolution is a myth, raising the question, "Why aren't monkeys still evolving into humans?" This is like arguing that erosion is a myth because the Himalayas are not still eroding into the Grand Canyon right before our eyes.

455

Who should one vote for, a candidate who dishonestly states what one wants to hear, or a candidate who *truthfully* states what one *does not* want to hear?

456

Do not let your corporate employer fool you: to it, you are nothing more than an undifferentiated, replaceable part.

457

One person's ignorance may be bliss—but it is typically not so blissful for that person's family, friends, and compatriots.

458

The most harmful aspect of marijuana to our nation is not usage; rather, it is the millions of criminal prosecutions *for* usage.

459

If the consequence for bringing our troops home from Iraq and Afghanistan is that some imbeciles will call us losers, so be it.

460

Despite all their claims, most Tea Partiers are libertarians only to the same extent that most Republicans are humanitarians (i.e., up to the point that any conflict with their *real* agenda arises).

461

From 2003 through 2006, Republicans had it all—the presidency, the House, the Senate, and the Supreme Court. Did they use this across-the-board authority to significantly deter abortions? Did they outlaw same-sex unions? Did they pass any legislation that noticeably improved our "family values"? No, they kept none of their promises, which were clearly lip service. The GOP's never-ending, insincere crusade against "immorality" is just a politically inexpensive way to buy the votes of conservative Christians.

462

In 1980, the GOP formed a coalition with the social conservative faction—thereby bestowing life to Frankenstein. Exploiting the strength of this creature, the GOP took numerous elections—and with each win, it falsely pledged *future* spoils to its ally. As the decades passed, however, Frankenstein grew ever more anxious from seldom receiving its due. In the end, seeing that it would never get its wishes met by playing along, Frankenstein vowed to wrest power from its partner's hands. And thus the Tea Party emerged.

463

If an imprudent man willfully smashes everything in a neighbor's home and—having no success in cleaning up his mess—enlists a "surge" of servants to restore a semblance of order, he does not end up meriting gratitude for any eventual successes in patching up his ill-advised destruction. *Is that not right, Dubya?*

464

We often hear that we must not suppress our emotions. This does not mean, however, that we are supposed to vent all of them without restraint. For example, regardless of how furious we are, it is *never* acceptable for us to rage abusively at another.

465

Science does not kill people. Unregulated capitalists *armed with science* kill people.

466

Carl Paladino—the Tea Party-backed millionaire who won the GOP gubernatorial nomination for New York—said that he would turn some prisons into dormitories for welfare recipients, where they would labor in state-sponsored "jobs," with former guards acting as their "counselors." He then added, "These are beautiful properties with basketball courts, bathroom facilities, toilet facilities.

Many young people would love to get the hell out of cities." Is this the aristocrats' scheme for handling our worsening poverty crisis? Will they use their overgrown prison system to "house" Americans who are guilty of nothing besides being poor? It sounds like an outlandish idea now—but it may not after several more years of the GOP raiding our public budgets for upper-income tax breaks.

467

If Carl Paladino did put welfare recipients in remodeled prisons, it would supposedly be done on a voluntary basis. However, is one truly "volunteering" if the only other option is to starve in an alley? Without a humane choice, *there is no choice.*

468

With genetically modified foods, a biotechnology company has the right to keep its "trade secrets" confidential—*and we have the right to never eat its unnatural, shadowy concoctions.*

469

If a biotechnology company insists that its genetically modified foods (crops or animals) are identical to traditional foods, and therefore do not need distinct labeling, *then it should lose its food patents because they are evidently not very novel.*

470

The invisible hand of the market is a pickpocket of workers.

471

Politicians will keep feeding us negative campaign ads, for they are what our Jerry Springer society most likes to consume.

472

Regarding negative campaigning, there is an enormous ethical difference between hurling mud and telling relevant truths. The difficulty lies in identifying which is which.

473

If Dick Cheney ran for president, it would be proper to place a barrage of "negative" campaign ads against him—and it would be wrong to permit him to dodge his record by whining about "unjust" mudslinging. Past behaviors are the surest indicators of future behaviors, and are fair game in any campaign.

474

When a society is in doubt about which course of action to take, it should always err on the side of compassion.

475

Republicans unveiled their "Pledge to America" yesterday, and House Minority Leader John Boehner aptly summarized it: "The point we make in this preamble to our pledge, is that we are not going to be any different than what we've been." This statement rates as one of the worst sales pitches in the history of politics.

476

We shoot ourselves in the foot whenever we surrender anything in negotiations with card-carrying members of the "party of no."

477

Since workers, like employers, are essential participants within an economy, a *sincere* free market capitalist should not have any philosophical issues with collective bargaining for the creation of labor contracts. They are just another form of transaction.

478

If a foreign nation had wrongfully detained and abused me for a long period, I would support attempts to topple the responsible government. It is a safe bet that foreigners feel likewise.

479

The GOP can have every Blue Dog Democrat: since it already picks up most of their key legislative votes, it might as well own all the blame arising from these votes. Indeed, Tea Partiers will know best how to handle this unfaithful breed of dog.

480

There are few Holocaust deniers compared to the masses that deny *other* holocausts—particularly the American-made ones.

481

You exist. God does not. It is more perfect to exist than not to exist. Therefore, you are more perfect (i.e., greater) than God.

482

In the long run, Tea Partiers will gravely wound the GOP. We can only pray that America does not suffer too much collateral damage along the way.

483

So how many collateral deaths to *American* civilians would we accept if a foreign "liberation" or "peacekeeping" operation were to occur on our soil? The answer is surely much smaller than the hundreds of thousands of innocent people that have died because of our military operations in countries such as Vietnam, Cambodia, Afghanistan, and Iraq.

484

Two persons can be "friends with benefits" —but only if neither of them tries to levy "taxes" on the other's benefits.

485

I do not mind admitting that I was incorrect, for by so doing, I acknowledge that I am now more enlightened than ever before.

486

The International Monetary Fund is the loan shark of free market capitalists: it provides loans to desperate countries—binding them to harsh conditionalities like deregulation, privatization, anti-protectionism, resource extraction, and austerity budgeting.

487

Priests now mostly side with "leftists" in foreign conflicts. *Does this mean that our war on communism is also a war on Christianity?*

488

Even if you decide to never get involved with politics, sooner or later it will decide to get involved with you.

489

Given the Democratic and Republican domination of our federal government and the polarization of the parties, a congressional candidate's political affiliation is more important than every other consideration combined. It is as if only two people are controlling Congress; we can either give one of them sufficient strength to lead, or abide gridlock. In reality, the sole factor that matters is the quantity—not the quality—of a party's components.

490

If you cannot understand national politics enough to know how to vote, ask yourself if you are wealthy: if yes, vote Republican; otherwise, vote Democrat. It really is that simple.

491

We forge aspiring soldiers into tools of combat. The ideal tool does not cogitate or practice free will: it merely functions as wielded. It is wise to remember that we do not ask a hammer how to build a house or blame it when we screw up the task.

492

The ultraconservative Fox *Propaganda* is correct when it says that all other news networks are liberal—*but only in comparison to it.*

493

One person's right to practice a religion never trumps another's right to speak against that religion and anything it holds sacred. If such open discussion offends worshippers, their faith is clearly too fragile or too un-American.

494

God took credit for every mystery of the universe, giving simple answers to primitive minds. Sadly, as humanity unravels each of these mysteries one by one, God refuses to make way for truth.

495

When we cripple our government, we cripple ourselves.

496

Though we have some say in our government, we have almost none in our corporate boardrooms; hence, as corporatism waxes, democracy wanes.

497

"It also took a long time to start slavery. And it started small, and it started with seemingly innocent ideas. And then a little court order here and a court order there, and a little more regulation here and a little more regulation there, and before we knew it, America had slavery. It didn't come over in a ship to begin with, as an evil slave trade. The government began to regulate things because the people needed answers and needed solutions. It started in a courtroom then it went to the legislatures. That's how slavery began. And it took a long time to enslave an entire race of people, and convince another race of people that they were somehow or another, less than them." Glenn Beck, the Fox *Propaganda* "historian," spewed these words on his radio show a week ago. By hacking and twisting the historical record in ways that anybody with a passable education can see, he shifted the culpability for slavery from greedy owners to *our* government. The true history of American slavery boils down to a single fact: aristocrats gamed the system to get away with murder—as they still do today.

498

In 2005 and 2006, Citigroup—one of the world's largest banks— published two research reports for investors, in which it coined the term "plutonomy"—an economy powered by the wealthy.

In these reports, researchers pointed out that "the U.S., UK, and Canada are world leaders in plutonomy." The rich in America "continue to account for a disproportionately large share of income and wealth" and they "are likely to get even wealthier in the coming years" at "the expense of labor." However, there is a significant threat endangering this plutonomy: the working class does not wield "much economic power, but it does have equal voting power with the rich." With their votes, the masses could strike back by hiking up the top tax rates. Since the "balance of power between right (generally pro-plutonomy) and left (generally pro-equality) is on a knife-edge," a "backlash against plutonomy is probable at some point." *This is our economic situation, straight from the horse's mouth.*

499

When fighting management, minimize friendly fire casualties.

500

Since no one can prove the existence of God, do not taint public debates by citing his equally unprovable words and deeds.

501

Everyone within our interwoven society—at some time, in some way—will be a "freeloader." Most conservatives, however, are unaware of this certainty. Consequently, when they strive to cut public programs and services, they are often proactively slicing their own throats.

502

The approximately 47% of us who pay no federal income tax will happily start doing so as soon as our exploitative aristocrats start paying us living wages.

503

Employers use cafeteria plans for benefits primarily as a way to slash perks and shift costs slowly and almost imperceptibly. Do we truthfully want to use the same process to divvy up public services like police protection and firefighting? (And if we did, could I opt out of paying for corporate welfare and the military?)

504

On paper, libertarian plans to minimize our government's role in serving society might look appealing; but in actual practice, the plans would spawn an immoral anarchy that only Satan and his moneyed followers could ever relish.

505

The victors do write our histories—but so do the losers: they just do not have as many publishers for their own biased works.

506

The bestowing of the Nobel Peace Prize on President Barack Obama said much less about him than it did about President George W. Bush.

507

When you are afraid of doing the wrong thing, do not reflexively select inaction. After all, inaction is itself an action.

508

Right-wing think tanks, unlike traditional ones, do not search for truth. Instead, they contrive specious arguments to advance their agenda. Put simply, right-wing think tanks *manufacture* "truth."

509

When breaking up with someone, be strong and decent enough to do it yourself. In particular, do not goad your soon-to-be ex into initiating the break; such deceit would cheat both of you out of any positive sentiments and memories that might otherwise survive.

510

In America's fascist subculture, Mexicans are the newest Jews.

511

Just as groups flourish by embracing diverse people, so too does an individual.

512

Birds of a feather that always flock together wind up with lives that are much too drab and limited.

513

In the universe of George W. Bush apologists, in which year does the blame for every problem shift from Clinton to Obama?

514

Even if homosexuality is a "choice," *everyone has the freedom to choose their own path in life*—at least until the big government of the GOP interferes.

515

I am not sexually attracted to some women, those with particular physical traits. This is natural. Though I could have dated them, I would have always found them to be physically unappealing. Put differently, such pursuits would have been *un*natural for me. We all make these "choices" when seeking a partner—*and for a homosexual, the natural choice is never the unappealing member of the opposite sex.*

516

Asking a homosexual to be heterosexual is like asking a dude who prefers beach babes to date only crippled, obese crones.

517

Jews who condone persecution, especially of homosexuals, need to reacquaint themselves with the history of Nazi Germany.

518

In a homophobic speech, Carl Paladino said, "I didn't march in a ... gay pride parade this year. My opponent did." Perhaps Carl could not be there because he was too busy e-mailing more of his bestiality videos.

519

The surest way for us to move our country past the persecution of homosexuals is to promptly give them equal rights. It is but a question of time before they get these rights; yet, until then—as we go on debating subjects like the "don't ask, don't tell" policy and same-sex marriage—emotions will remain intense. We must legally acknowledge homosexual equality, get this issue out of sight and out of mind, and begin societal assimilation.

520

For centuries, Christians have persecuted numerous peoples. As soon as it falls out of vogue to crucify one group, Christianity targets another. Its current victims are homosexuals. For good or ill, Christianity is America's primary ethical engine—and the driving force behind anti-gay bigotry. *Will Christians prove to be any better than Muslims are at policing their own terrorists?*

521

Across the country, Tea Party candidates are campaigning to kill the same governmental programs that assisted them in the past. Since they are not pressing to revamp or replace these programs, they must believe that such public aid is unnecessary. This makes them either greedy freeloaders or selfish hypocrites—depending on whether or not they had really needed their own previously accepted aid.

522

Our widely criticized, inhumane embargo of Cuba seems to have no remaining justification besides ensuring the complete failure of the country's economic and political policies. Owing to Uncle Sam's fear that Cuban ideology will contaminate his workers, he continues to "sterilize" the island. *He will never let us witness any communistic success stories.*

523

In George Orwell's novel, *1984*, the Party employs three slogans: war is peace, freedom is slavery, and ignorance is strength. As I read this book, I cannot shake the feeling that I am studying the official field manual of the GOP and Fox *Propaganda*.

524

During yesterday's debate, Christine O'Donnell sidestepped the question of whether she still maintains evolution is a myth by saying, "Local schools should make that decision." This clichéd answer demonstrates how we wrongly empower state and local governments: since O'Donnell knows our national government will never endorse her imbecilic science opinions, she wants to place all judgments in the hands of innumerable school boards; at least some of them will force-feed her nonsense to students. The truths of science do not vary from town to town—*but the understanding of science does*, thanks to our schizophrenic system for governing schools.

525

We should never cherry-pick scientific facts based on popularity or how good they make us feel—as we do with religious beliefs.

526

There is one crucial difference between the political donations made by unions and those made by corporations: unions give money raised from participating members, while corporations give money raised from *non*participating *customers* (i.e., we all pay —*unknowingly*—for corporate campaign spending via higher prices).

527

There is a stronger consensus among relevant experts regarding the danger posed by global warming than there ever was regarding the danger posed by Saddam Hussein. Still—even though we passively followed our warlords into Iraq, wasting hundreds of billions of dollars—we never cease to call into question the integrity and agendas *of our scientists*. It appears that the only consensuses that count are the ones our military alarmists are fabricating.

528

It is not the educated elite that we must be wary of, but rather the *wealthy* elite.

529

God is the quintessential dictator—and atheists are humanity's boldest freedom fighters.

530

Unprivileged youths will attend sabotaged public schools. Then, in adulthood, they will compete in an ever more exploitative job market. And when their survival becomes too arduous and bleak, they will "volunteer" to serve the military-industrial complex, dying in wars of imperialism. *This is the well-trodden life path that the GOP has mapped out for us commoners.*

531

An individualist can only be as free as *any* of the stronger will allow.

532

News Corp. followed up its $1 million donation to the Republican Governors Association with $250,000 more—and an extra political gift of $1 million to the U.S. Chamber of Commerce (aka corporate America). Rupert Murdoch justified his influencing of elections with shareholder funds by claiming, "It's certainly in the interest of the country ... that there be a ... fair amount of change in Washington." If the father of Fox *Propaganda* feels this strongly about putting conservatives back in charge, one is naive to believe that his child is not supporting him by using its loud, persuasive voice to peddle right-wing punditry instead of news.

533

At the annual meeting of News Corp., upset shareholders grilled Rupert Murdoch (aka Emperor Palpatine) over his generous and unprecedented political donations. Voicing a concern of many, one investor asked Murdoch if he would be willing to involve the shareholders in determining any future gifts. He responded, "No. Sorry, you have the right to vote us off the board if you don't like that." His answer sounds fair until one learns that the Murdoch family owns enough voting stock to make it virtually impossible to wrest control from him. This situation illustrates the manner of democracy that our plutocrats wish to implement in America.

534

Two weeks ago, Rush Limbaugh claimed, "Some people are just born to be slaves." Is he referring to the exploited citizens who are misguidedly voting for Republicans, the toadies of our corporate masters? These voters must start reading between his lines—and stop shackling themselves at the ballot box.

535

If markets pay some workers too much (e.g., hedge fund managers) or too little (e.g., teachers), taxes are the best adjustment tools.

536

The solution to one person's problem may not solve anything on a societal level. For example, swearing an oath of abstinence may keep a particular girl from getting pregnant; yet, when millions of girls try the same approach, a certain percentage will still end up pregnant. If the resulting number of teen pregnancies is too high, this "solution" is unviable for an entire society.

537

If the economic policies of Republicans are so effective, why do we find our nation's highest poverty rates within *red* states?

538

There is a sure way to dissuade Congress from rashly throwing us into war: we could require every member who actively backs a military action to supply a blood relative for duty on the front lines. (Naturally, we could enforce such a reasonable plan only in fantasyland.)

539

When public figures lie, call them liars in public.

540

In Christine O'Donnell's most recent debate, she smugly asked her opponent, "Where in the Constitution is the separation of church and state?" When he answered that the First Amendment spells it all out, O'Donnell expressed her skepticism. As with other Tea Partiers—the self-declared guardians of our Constitution—she knows even less about its text than a fifth grader does. Just as I will not place my body in the hands of would-be healers who got their schooling exclusively from ignorant quacks, I will not place my Constitution in the hands of would-be lawmakers who got their schooling exclusively from ignorant fascists.

541

It is deceitful to say that the "separation of church and state" is not in the First Amendment; it is like saying that our "right to own *guns*" is not in the Second Amendment. Though we cannot see the precise phrases, the full concepts are clearly visible.

542

If our founders had truly intended to create a Christian nation, why does Article VI of our Constitution state that "no religious

Test shall ever be required as a Qualification to any Office or public Trust under the United States"?

543

Most atheists could write a better list of commandments than the one Moses delivered.

544

When people commit violent acts, they normally lie about some of the details. Thus, we should trust very little of what military leaders say in wartime: they have many violent deeds to conceal and an ignoble tradition of misinforming civilians.

545

The GOP has perfected the art of blaming the victim.

546

In a libertarian nation, all needy people must resort to beggary to survive. Besides being barbaric, this is also an inefficient use of labor resources (e.g., without public healthcare, I would always be busy looking for ways to stay alive—rather than writing this book).

547

Although class warfare is intrinsic to all capitalist systems, our aristocrats publicly condemn its practice by anyone. They do so to promote false truces that lower our defenses, for it is far easier for them to win the war when they can launch frequent covert attacks. Before it is too late, we must realize that the wealthy are waging economic warfare without quarter; that we are losing rapidly; and that if we fall, America will fall with us.

548

Our aristocrats are playing a dangerous game of class warfare, a game they cannot win: if they keep pushing us over the edge, in the end we will reflexively drag them with us into the abyss.

549

If we legalize drugs across North America, the drug cartels will move on to other business endeavors, just as the mafia did after the repeal of Prohibition. And though these new ventures might also be illegal, they could scarcely instigate the same amount of violence that comes with drug trafficking.

550

It is hard to get American men to properly honor fatherhood when our culture and courts are not granting them the same rights and respect that mothers customarily receive.

551

A private firm *might* beat a public agency in efficiency—but *only* if the firm operates in a legitimately competitive environment.

552

If you really believe that voting is for "losers," then you truly have no excuse for not being the first loser in line at the ballot box.

553

The success of Scientology demonstrates how easy it is to create a religion. Its claim that we are all eternally reincarnated aliens known as Thetans (who willed themselves into existence *trillions* of years ago) earns the derision of nearly everyone—and this is merely the first layer of silliness. While others will question how such a crazy cult could attract so many devout believers, I instead wonder how often Abraham and his religious descendants have evoked the very same question over the last 3500-odd years.

554

Unlike Democrats, Republicans gear their messages for simple minds. Given that the GOP usually wins messaging wars, what conclusions can we draw concerning the strength of the typical American mind?

555

For our nation's benefit, the GOP again wants to defund public television and radio stations. If they lose government funding, many will go under or become the indebted tools of corporate America. Only with Republican "logic" can one make the case that the strangulation of our non-corporate voices will somehow be good for us.

556

We should slash the tax rates for corporations by 50% — *but only after they have forfeited all of their tax breaks and loopholes.*

557

Although most conservatives act like they are macho, they are in truth cowards for they are terrified of nearly everything outside their doors.

558

Right-wingers are our nation's foremost philosophical idealists: their subjective perceptions constitute all of their realities.

559

In a recent interview, Senate GOP leader Mitch McConnell said, "The single most important thing we want to achieve is for President Obama to be a one-term president." I reckon that many individuals who plan to vote Republican next week would be dismayed to learn that the repair of our economy is not the top priority of the GOP.

560

It is easy to criticize something that one knows nothing about.

561

Christine O'Donnell now contends that she is a victim of sexism: "There's no doubt that they wouldn't say the things they're saying about me, they wouldn't do the things that they're doing if I weren't a woman." No, Christine, we treat you like an imbecile because you are deplorably ignorant. And by falsely charging discrimination, *you are discrediting legitimate victims of sexism* — which leads to the empowerment of bigots.

562

Regarding evildoings, religious fundamentalists are the ultimate practitioners of projection.

563

A note to all the bad parents of the world: no matter what God says, procreation by itself should never earn an offspring's honor.

564

There is a promising technique for deprogramming the fans of Fox *Propaganda*: urge them to watch *The Daily Show with Jon Stewart*.

As a side benefit, studies have shown that they would be joining a much better educated and informed audience.

565

It is a bad sign for our fourth estate when television newscasts provide no more substance than "fake news" programs like *The Daily Show* and *The Colbert Report*.

566

When wealthy entrepreneurs hold their excess capital, electing to forego new business opportunities, there is only one credible reason: there is too little consumer demand to justify additional products or services. Supplying entrepreneurs extra money via lower tax rates will not address this lack of demand. Rather, it would just hand them more unnecessary treasures to horde.

567

Angry and frightened people are the soil from which fascism sprouts.

568

Tea Partiers are not Nazis; they are Nazi enablers.

569

The private sector finances job creation by borrowing, utilizing savings, cutting costs, or raising prices on customers—just as the public sector finances job creation by borrowing, utilizing surpluses, cutting spending, or raising taxes on citizens. One can bicker over which sector best serves the particular needs of a society, but it is obvious that both of them—through comparable financial methods—create jobs. And a job is a job is a job.

570

A year ago, Corrections Corporation of America (CCA) wrote that it would get "a significant portion" of its future revenues from U.S. Immigration and Customs Enforcement. How could the company ensure that this forecast would be accurate? First, it assisted in drafting Arizona's immigration bill. Then CCA teamed up with other prison companies to employ lobbyists and award "donations" to 30 of the 36 bill co-sponsors—using cash earned from public contracts (i.e., taxpayer funds). Governor Brewer—acting with two chief advisors who had been prison company lobbyists—promptly signed the bill, and a national movement was started. Later on, the president of CCA said, "I can only believe the opportunities at the federal level are going to continue apace as a result of what's happening. Those people coming across the border and getting caught are going to have to be detained and ... there's going to be enhanced opportunities for what we do." This series of events demonstrates how unbridled capitalism is eroding civil liberties and buying democracy right under our noses.

571

When a political party manages to marginalize all other parties, tyranny inevitably follows. The same rule applies to countries: since the collapse of the Soviet Union, America has economically and militarily strong-armed the international community to an even greater degree. *Maybe the world needs a second superpower—like China—to give us some ideological competition and to keep us honest.*

572

With every twisting of reality that Christian leaders execute in their efforts to peddle unscientific absurdities that are on par with Earth being at the center of the universe—*I notice myself increasingly questioning* all *teachings of the church.*

573

Someday I will prove the existence of God. I will finagle this by first blogging, "Scientists have recently proved God's existence." Then I will entice Fox *Propaganda* commentators into referencing my fake "news" as a fact to back their opinions. Afterward, Fox *Propaganda* newscasters will report extensively on the viral talk that the scientific breakthrough has roused. Other news outlets will follow suit, not wanting to look like they are out of touch — or atheists. Some people will eventually discredit the story by exposing my blog as its source, but few will hear their message: any retractions will be muted to minimize embarrassment. And my "proof" will live on as truth in the minds of the misinformed.

574

A population that can believe in creationism can also believe in any falsehood, no matter how outrageous, that Fox *Propaganda* spreads.

575

The United Nations is just a lapdog on a leash that is "leading" its master, the United States of America.

576

There is only one real reason that nations initiate wars: to satisfy the desires of their rulers. Any other reasons that historians give are simply the pretexts that rulers have used to rally people onto battlefields.

577

The charade of eliminating the nearly mythical cases of voter fraud facilitates the GOP's rampant practice of voter suppression.

578

We cannot confirm the validity of *any* moral principle. Not only is it impossible to prove whether a particular act is inherently good or evil, it is similarly impossible to verify that good and evil even exist. And so—just as we are free to choose a religion—we should be equally free to choose our own ethical system. The issue is a matter of personal preference, not scientific law.

579

The recording of an ethical system within "holy" books or statutes does not universally bestow intrinsic moral worth to any action.

580

Even if you are free to live by any ethical values, your conduct must not interfere with the freedom of others to do the same.

581

To maximize liberty, the cornerstone of America, our laws must not impinge on the freedom of people to follow their own ethical beliefs—except to ensure that nobody's resultant actions inhibit others from exercising their own ethical freedoms.

582

Does any billionaire truly work 10,000 times harder than you do?

583

All citizens should have the right to consume and abuse *anything* (e.g., food, drink, drugs). If, however, this consumption leads directly to someone else's harm, we must punish harshly. One is free to harm oneself, *but never others*.

584

It is unethical to hoard and consume *excessive* shares of limited resources, for such conduct hurts others by forcing them to live with less than they are due. *This principle applies most commonly to questions regarding divisions of wealth.*

585

Life is like a game: it is difficult to be a winner if one does not know all the rules—as well as how to work around them.

586

When you meet an obstacle in life, it is not always necessary to tackle it: sometimes you just need to resolutely take a detour.

587

The phrase "the will of the people" does not sound as legitimate and wholesome when one rewords it as "the will of the mob."

588

The more aggressively a salesperson sells unworthy wares, the quicker the devil will purchase that person's soul.

589

Sarah Palin's books, *Going Rogue* and *America by Heart*, come in a handful of convenient formats: one-ply, two-ply, and three-ply.

590

Most major tax reform endeavors are well-disguised acts of class warfare, perpetrated by the affluent to redistribute wealth.

591

The Pentagon is not really worried about what our enemies might learn from the WikiLeaks military files; *it is far more worried about what everyone else might discover.* After all, our enemies already know of the many wrongs that our leaders have committed. But if Americans and their allies find out....

592

It is clear that Obama looks like a socialist—*if you are a fascist.*

593

Being pro-choice does not necessarily make one pro-abortion.

594

To create temporary public commissions that are more capable, we should no longer staff them with appointees. Instead, we should utilize a lottery system as we do with juries. A random citizen is a surer bet than a political puppet.

595

Ever since the day when God forbade Adam to eat from the tree of knowledge, most religious leaders have kept their followers away from similar trees—much to the vexation of intellectuals.

596

While I support government spending for developing a healthy, educated workforce, right-wingers support substantially higher government spending for developing an unproductive, bloated military. Thus, *I am the genuine fiscal conservative*—and they are merely wasteful imposters.

597

Ignorant atheists and intellectual theists are equally uncommon.

598

Listening to adults discussing political issues is too often like listening to children discussing where babies come from.

599

We must remove unsuccessful teachers and raise salaries in their field to attract and keep better workers. Until schools can pay more, the best potential teachers will seek other work. As well-bred capitalists, we realize that one gets what one pays for — and so far, we have paid teachers peanuts, comparatively.

600

One can follow Jesus without being a Christian.

601

If Democrats bow to the recent 2010 mandate in the same way Republicans bowed to Obama's more sweeping 2008 mandate, I wonder how loudly the hypocritical GOP will scream treason.

602

The 2003 PISA report showed that in a math test of students from 40 countries, our scores were near the bottom — but in a measurement of our students' confidence in math, we finished at the top. With this unmerited arrogance, our students will see no deficiencies in their abilities. They will insist that they are learning enough. And when they then become adults, *they will join all the other swaggering Americans who also erroneously brag about exceptionalism.*

603

A crowd often makes one feel lonelier than an empty room does.

604

You are not required to be everyone's friend, but you should try to be friendly to everyone.

605

An illegal toxic waste site should become the maker's new home.

606

In paradise, no one must pay taxes. Regrettably, we do not live in paradise. At least some of us must pay. So whom do you wish to hand our country's bills to, the haves or the have-nots? You make the choice. A balanced budget awaits your decision.

607

Since it is safer and easier to commit murders by using contract killers, the Pentagon employs militia warriors around the globe to conquer "leftist" governments. Though it euphemistically calls these agents "freedom fighters" — *that which we call a contract killer, by any other name would smell as foul.*

608

When deists speak of God, they are merely reciting sappy poetry.

609

If you ever employ a group of people to carry out barbaric deeds (e.g., torture) and you are foolish enough to admit it in a book (e.g., George W. Bush's *Decision Points*), do not fret: you can still avoid prosecution by concocting a first-class excuse (e.g., your bootlicking lawyers assured you that your plan to order torture was legal).

610

To be a successful political prognosticator, never underestimate the power of money in a campaign or the gullibility of voters.

611

The pretexts for waging war have not changed within the last few centuries, as verified by Thomas Jefferson's words: "We believe no more in Bonaparte's fighting merely for the liberties of the seas, than in Great Britain's fighting for the liberties of mankind. The object of both is the same, to draw to themselves the power, the wealth, and the resources of other nations." Our greedy leaders still prod us onto foreign battlefields, where we suffer and die solely for the benefit of absent aristocrats. How many more centuries will pass before we understand that we are but pawns—and that we can ignore our king's false urgings by simply walking off the chessboard?

612

If we could renounce all religions, it would be worth it if only to deactivate the giant button that our leaders habitually push.

613

Today, the GOP ordered its first vote since the 2010 elections—an effort to defund NPR. House Minority Leader Eric Cantor led the assault, stating that he did not wish "to fund news organizations with a partisan point of view." Do Republicans truly want our government to penalize news outlets that do not pass someone's political litmus test? If so, I should point out that there are many ways for both parties to practice censorship—and that NPR regularly polls ahead of Fox *Propaganda* in trustworthiness and neutrality.

614

Individual freedom comes at a price that many people do not really want to pay: responsibility for one's choices.

615

Whenever you quit struggling for your liberties, you are locking slave chains around your own neck.

616

In a hearing to address full-body scans and pat-down searches at airports, Senator John Ensign asked if there would be a religious exemption for the procedures. The reply was no, appropriately: *religious people instigated this entire mess, and they are the likeliest candidates to carry out the next terrorist attack*. If there is to be an exemption, it should be for *non*religious flyers.

617

Over the last decade, we had accepted unconstitutional searches of our bags, luggage, clothing, property, vehicles, homes, phone calls, e-mails, etc.—but as soon as someone patted and scanned our naughty parts, America cried foul. We are such prudes.

618

If you wish to immerse yourself in someone's religious dogma, so be it. Please, though, spare your children from indoctrination. Give them a chance to use their own minds—to freely discover what they themselves believe.

619

A religiously programmed child and a preacher's computer are equally pious.

620

I dread our inevitable knee-jerk overreaction to a terror attack by the soon-to-be-famous "anal cavity bomber."

621

If you feel inconvenienced at home by the war on terror, imagine how our misused troops in Iraq and Afghanistan feel.

622

From 9/12 onwards, we have been busy terrorizing ourselves.

623

How much would you value the love of someone who gives it to you only because of brainwashing? Most likely, God similarly values such "love" when *he* is its recipient.

624

I never said, "I think that people at the high end ... should be paying a lot more in taxes. We have it better than we've ever had it." And regarding claims that the wealthy need tax cuts to stimulate business activity, *I* did not say, "The rich are always going to say ... 'Just give us more money, and we'll go out and spend more, and then it will all trickle down to the rest of you.' But that has not worked the last 10 years, and I hope the American public is catching on." Nor did *I* push to preserve the estate tax by saying, "I think we need to ... take a little more out of the hides of guys like me." No, it was actually Warren Buffet, the world's third richest man, who spoke these words—and I will bow to *his* business knowledge and judgment.

625

MSNBC and Fox *Propaganda* are in opposition, but not because they have differing political viewpoints. Rather, it is because they handle the news differently: the former reports it and the latter *dis*torts it.

626

At the hands of Tea Partiers, moderate Republicans have become an endangered species. You can help pull these vital politicians back from the brink of extinction—by voting *Democrat*.

627

In the final quarter of 2010, American businesses took in record profits at an annualized rate of $1.68 trillion. Yet, corporate profiteers and their Republican agents ceaselessly criticize President Obama for being too anti-business. Something does not add up here.

628

The only real competition one will find in America is between us laborers. Since we are so worried about losing our jobs, we are undercutting each other, working harder and longer for less. Of course, as we fight like dogs for scraps, our masters are raking in all the profits from *our* heightened productivity.

629

How many people truly believe that Mark Zuckerberg deserves several billion dollars for his work on Facebook?

630

Owing to the idolatry of Tea Partiers, Sarah Palin is on a short list for the presidency and her daughter, Bristol, is a finalist on *Dancing with the Stars*. These accomplishments are due to the rabid backing of Palinites, not personal ability: Bristol continually receives low scores for her dancing, and Sarah's scores are even poorer for her thinking. *Clearly, Tea Partiers are advocates of affirmative action for unqualified rednecks.*

631

Afghanistan is a grease fire and our military is water. So what do you think will happen when our generals splash additional soldiers into this frying pan? (Warning: do not attempt this at home.)

632

Despite what we always hear, the GOP does not really support our troops; rather, it supports the production of war machines. The GOP constantly offers good lip service to the troops, but raises to their wages and benefits come mostly from Democratic efforts. This will not change unless the GOP sees a way to raise business profits via spending on military personnel. Until then, it will continue to treat the labor component of our armed forces only a bit better than it would treat a necessary welfare program.

633

Adults need God as much as children need Santa.

634

Until we melt down all of our cultural heritages in the American pot, racists will keep feeding off our celebrated differences.

635

America's secrets are less a byproduct of national security than they are of efforts to ensure governmental *job* security.

636

Liberals and conservatives must negotiate a truce in their social war so that they can target their true oppressor: the aristocracy.

637

For the sake of fairness and balance, I now give George W. Bush a compliment: he reminds me of Albert Einstein and the Dalai Lama—whenever I compare him to Sarah Palin.

638

We would all be healthier living with sobering truths instead of feel-good fantasies. The former are potent remedies, the latter just placebos. Fantasies deceive us, making us believe that they are effective and essential—as they secretly enfeeble our psyches.

639

If we shift to implement middle-of-the-road policies (*as defined by the Tea Party*), we will actually end up *mud bogging* in a far-right ditch—a sport that offers loads of fun for rednecks, but would leave our country in a helluva mess.

640

In my lifetime as a Medicaid recipient, I have repeatedly fought life-threatening cuts to coverage. These cuts have always been budgeted by the hands of *Republican*-controlled state government. This should surprise no one: who is most likely to slash public expenditures for our safety nets, a "bleeding-heart" Democrat or a "fiscally responsible" Republican? *I have found your government "death panels," Sarah—and their members come entirely from your own cold-blooded party!*

641

Work does suck, but by daily making a realistic list of tasks to complete, one can transform drudgery into a rewarding contest.

642

On Rush Limbaugh's recent show, he asked, "If people cannot even feed and clothe themselves, should they be allowed to vote?" He then suggested that the greed of these struggling people debases their votes. If this is a valid point (which it is not), we must also question the votes of greedy multimillionaires like Limbaugh (e.g., since his net income will be over $1 million greater each year if Congress extends the Bush-era tax cuts, are we sure that *his* latest votes reflected what was best for our country?). In truth, Limbaugh is simply campaigning for his fellow aristocrats: *they would love to reinstate property ownership requirements for voting.* If we lose our right to vote because we own too little, the wealthy will no longer need to dupe us into supporting their causes. America will at last belong totally to them.

643

If you collect all of the rottenest parts of politicians, stitch them together into one being, and stuff it full of steroids, you end up with Sarah Palin. This she-monster is not one of us.

644

Believers see the world as it "should" work, while true scholars see the world as it *does* work.

645

President Obama surrendered today, agreeing to pay ransom to our aristocrats. Their foot soldiers in the GOP threatened to hold America hostage by blocking all legislation until we ceded tax cuts to millionaires—billions of dollars that *we* will shortly be forced to pay for through reduced services or increased taxes. So once again, we lost because nobody is fighting hard enough for us. I fear that if our leaders do not start doing so, we citizens will have no choice but to march on Washington—*to make them take our side.*

646

Sarah Palin could save Barack Obama's presidency, and perhaps our nation: she would just need to allow surgeons to transplant her misused cohones into him, thereby replacing his atrophied pair.

647

A wise person forgives—but only a fool forgets.

648

The juvenile way that our nation is handling its economic problems should scare the crap out of foreigners, for when we go down, we will certainly drag everyone in the world along with us.

649

With our nation's aging population, declining middle class, and deteriorating environment, we will unavoidably enter a depression, sooner rather than later. When we crash, unequaled anarchy will plague us: modern Americans—being more ill-suited than ever to cope with extreme levels of poverty—will too frequently wind up killing for soup instead of working for it. Rebellious people may welcome such a future, but their bravados will be short-lived once they realize that the revolts do not look like the ones glamorized in Hollywood movies.

650

Given that reason is a best friend to democracy, and that Martin Luther stated, "Reason is the greatest enemy that faith has," we can surmise that faith and democracy do not have much warmth for each other.

651

The Catholic Church damns gay men for refusing to procreate with women and blesses priests for doing exactly the same. *This fine line is undoubtedly tripping many confused men into seminary closets.*

652

Lazy Christians venerate faith ahead of good works because it is easier to preach a belief than to practice one. A bit more effort put into good works would make faith a little less cheap.

653

There is a formidable organization within America that is openly plotting insurrection. One of its leaders, Randall Terry, said, "We are called by God to conquer this country." To do this, the rebel group is following an insidious, long-term plan to subvert our children: as two more of its leaders, James Dobson and Gary Bauer, wrote, "Those who control what young people are taught and what they experience—what they see, hear, think, and believe—will determine the future course for the nation." Many incriminating quotes similar to these exist, detailing the continuing efforts of the combatants in this group to take over our country bit by bit. If they were Muslims, they would never have the numbers to succeed; nevertheless, we would register them as terrorists, exposing and thwarting their activities. *So why are we ignoring the un-American schemes of this organized horde of* Christian *fundamentalists?*

654

Show me a fundamentalist spouting "facts" in a political debate, and I will show you a habitual liar.

655

As you age, you will regularly learn about the deaths of people you have known in one way or another. Do not grieve; instead, pay tribute to them by treasuring every remaining day of your own unique life.

656

One can cheat death for years by staying too busy to die.

657

On your private property, you are free to behave as bigotedly as you desire; however, once you open your property to conduct business with the public, their human rights always supersede your freedom to act abusively.

658

If you refuse to donate organs, why should you ever receive one?

659

When a man and woman get intoxicated together, they should share the blame for all of their resulting stupidities.

660

The sexes will never be equal as long as we condone our criminal justice system's universal presupposition that all males are carnal predators—and all females are merely their fragile, chaste victims.

661

If whistleblowers are terrorists, America is now a police state.

662

The U.S. Chamber of Commerce represents small businesses as much as the United Nations represents small town councils.

663

Pornographers, prostitutes, and strippers do not act as pressure cookers. Rather, they serve as release valves.

664

A feminist who works to liberate women from men's shackles, only to swap them with others of her own design, is not truly a feminist: she is a hypocritical turncoat.

665

Many people condemn prostitution for its buying and selling of working girls. So why are we not also condemning temporary employment agencies for operating as exploitative pimps?

666

With Julia Roberts as a hooker and Richard Gere as her john, we get the makings of a fashionably romantic tale. If, however, we recast these sexy stars with two everyday, plain-looking people, we end up with—in the eyes of many individuals—an immoral crime. In fact, the uglier the participants are, the harsher our society judges them and *any* sex acts they perform. Hence, I am driven to fight this discrimination: though I am not one of the "beautiful" people, *my sexual activities are no less wholesome or proper.*

667

Prostitution is akin to illegal drugs: the ills associated with it arise principally from its criminalization, not its practice.

668

At the end of time, the last humans will still be using outlawed drugs as they engage in outlawed sex.

669

In 1941, as we planned for our possible entry into World War II, President Franklin Roosevelt signed the May Act. The law banned prostitution near military bases, and it demonstrated a hallmark of American culture: we will unhesitatingly permit thousands of our troops to experience the agony of war, but not the ecstasy of sex. Evidently, hookers were a graver threat than Nazis.

670

In order to promote a fake image of wholesomeness, Las Vegas has prohibited prostitution since 1971. Nonetheless, prostitutes continue to play major roles in Sin City's dealings—so much so that many visitors believe prostitution is still legal there, as it is in nearby counties. So what did this city of vice reap from its futile efforts to hoodwink families, other than the sexual diseases and crimes that are rarely found within the areas of Nevada where prostitution remains legal and highly regulated? *Las Vegas won no societal benefits*—just as the rest of America has with its own ban on paid sex.

671

A prostitute cannot break a marriage that is already broken from the weight of unmet needs; on the other hand, a prostitute might —by meeting these needs—keep such a marriage glued together.

672

When I was a corporate accountant, my employer exploited my mind and destroyed my self-esteem; the degradation and soul-numbing work nearly gave me a nervous breakdown. Since I am confident that I am not the only accountant who has had such an experience, maybe we should prohibit this line of work. After all, we have a duty to protect all "bean counters" from *brain* exploitation—even if many of them do not really feel very demeaned and have few other career options that pay so well.

673

Owing to my disease, my body has been broken since childhood. I was reassured back then that our minds are more important than our bodies, and this conviction has consoled me through the years. But there has always been an inconsistency with it: if minds are truly more important, why does our society protect only bodies—the fittest ones—from exploitation? The reality is that most people value a good body over a good brain.

674

Opponents of the sex industry often attack it for treating women like objects. This is a meaningless criticism: as I learned in grade school English, it is always incorrect to treat people like verbs.

675

If people continually denigrated your profession, you would most likely find your work to be more degrading than it truly is.

676

The more loudly society condemns the sex industry, the more degradingly many individuals will treat sex workers, and the more self-destructively these workers will behave in response. *Condemnations frequently end up being self-fulfilling prophecies.*

677

Strippers generally find lonely old men to be remarkably polite in comparison to pretty frat boys. Most of the former treat the women like ladies, while the latter treat them like whores. This comes as a surprise to many first-time patrons: in their shallow eyes, it is the unattractive geezers, not the boys, who appear to be the dangerous predators we fear. *It is in this way that beauty deceives us, making us lower our defenses against the genuine threats.*

678

If money cannot buy happiness, neither can capitalism.

679

To get global warming deniers to be more accepting of the facts, we should use a label that better depicts how our new climate changes look to simpletons. Maybe "wacky weather" would work.

680

If Santa Claus were real, would we not harbor suspicions that he is a child molester who is stalking everyone's kids?

681

Since prostitution is illegal, why are we not banning marriages between filthy rich geezers and large-breasted bimbos?

682

Democrats are to Republicans as dreamers are to schemers.

683

Corporations are eager to snatch up every government handout without any shame. Furthermore, our courts have declared that corporations are equal to people. Therefore, as loyal capitalists, we should never pass up a chance to greedily take government cash —copying the example set by our enlightened corporate brethren.

684

We now have yet another study showing that Fox *Propaganda* viewers, in comparison to consumers of other news sources, are the most misinformed. The University of Maryland conducted this study by surveying voters from the 2010 midterm elections, quizzing them on key campaign issues. With most of the issues, viewers of Fox *Propaganda* scored worst (consumers of MSNBC and public broadcasting typically scored best). More notably, unlike with other news sources, *greater exposure to Fox generated greater misinformation.* After the release of this study, a senior vice president for the network dismissed it by insinuating that the student researchers were lazy drunks—*which ironically was also misinformation.*

685

By sacrificing the fantasy of an afterlife, the valuation of your *life* appreciates—for it becomes a much rarer commodity.

686

If members of a large group convinced themselves that 2 + 2 = 5, why should anyone ever praise them for their strong faith rather than mock them for their disgraceful idiocy?

687

It takes much more courage to reject the feel-good beliefs of the popular crowd than it does to drink its "blessed" Kool-Aid.

688

For many persons who believe in Heaven, the threat of Hell is an oppressive cross that subconsciously crushes the spirit of life.

689

Those who shout loudest for tax cuts, privatization, or a leaner public sector should never complain when the government fails to provide a particular service.

690

Modern Republicans are a synthesis of affluence, heartlessness, and ignorance in various proportions.

691

Invisible con artists are robbing everyone on a daily basis. With no violence or house intrusions, they are stealing far more than traditional thieves ever could. But most victims are unaware of these losses since they cannot see the sharks in action. Hence, unlike with thieves, we rarely even try to deter them. We are so skeptical of the existence of their fraudulent deeds that we will deride anyone who merely seeks to point them out—for as well-bred capitalists, we must allow no one to besmirch our corporate crooks.

692

PolitiFact editors and reporters have chosen the 2010 Lie of the Year: "Obamacare" is "a government takeover of health care." The unearthing of orders from Fox *Propaganda's* vice president to its news staff to use the term "government-run health insurance" whenever possible leaves no doubt as to which network helped propagate the lie. So, knowing that this led to the neutering of the final legislation, how much additional suffering will we now need to attribute to Murdoch and his misinformation machine?

693

People who religiously disbelieve facts are unqualified to run businesses, organizations, political parties—and our country.

694

While many Capitol Hill Democrats occasionally lie, all of their Republican colleagues *habitually* lie. Without lies, the GOP has no effective approach for hawking its rapacious agenda.

695

There will rarely ever be masterful bank heists like those shown in Hollywood movies—for brilliant thieves know that it is much easier to steal wealth by incorporating fly-by-night businesses.

696

If I offered to lend you billions of dollars at 0% interest with the stipulation that I will pay you 2% interest to borrow it all back, would you describe the bargain as too good to be true? If so, you would be mistaken: it is essentially the same deal that our government has given Wall Street since the economic meltdown of 2008. It seems that if capitalists receive free public money through a "businessy" transaction, they are not welfare queens.

697

On the individual level, honesty and openness are not always the easiest options at the start, but they are consistently the best options by the end. *Perhaps world diplomacy would improve if we regularly heeded this truism when holding national level talks.*

698

St. Augustine wrote, "There is another form of temptation, even more fraught with danger. This is the disease of curiosity." I fear that many Christians still think likewise. Without curiosity, ignorance thrives—and though ignorance fortifies faith, it also suppresses the knowledge humans need to survive. We should note that St. Augustine inscribed these words at the dawn of the Dark Ages; let us pray that we will not soon be entering another.

699

There is at least one thing that is more oppressive than tyranny of the majority: tyranny of the *minority*.

700

An apology is worthless if its maker has no intention to correct the objectionable behavior.

701

A being that acts only in self-interest is no more evolved than the simplest of creatures.

702

The symbol for the GOP is an elephant—but it is inappropriate: unlike elephants, Republican voters *always* forget.

703

Perhaps Democrats should offer their symbol to the GOP: with its record-smashing use of the filibuster over the last two years of national turmoil, the "party of no" has surpassed every other entity in epitomizing the donkey (i.e., stubborn ass).

704

There is a surefire way to cut alcohol use and abuse: give us a healthier, safer option by legalizing marijuana. *Naturally, the alcohol industry will keep lobbying against this sensible plan.*

705

Politics would not be so confusing if the press would focus less on the sweet-sounding words of our legislators and more on their actual voting records.

706

The downturn in the housing market has hit even the White House: during the last three years, it has lost nearly a quarter of its value. I just hope that devious bankers do not accidentally-on-purpose foreclose on it—and thereby add President Obama's family to the growing list of wrongfully evicted tenants.

707

George W. Bush's administration crafted terrorism policies using Cheney's "one percent doctrine." Ron Suskind aptly defined this doctrine, writing, "Even if there's just a one percent chance of the unimaginable coming due, act as if it is a certainty." With global warming's potential to cause far more harm than all terrorists ever could, the same standard should obviously apply. So where is the matching trillion dollars for a war on *global warming*?

708

I have immense respect for our military personnel, who sacrifice so much for us for so little in return. Nevertheless, we should acknowledge that they are not all brainy saints. They are just like us, and it is unfair to judge them by criteria that we cannot live up to ourselves. Our warriors are not paid enough to be our role models.

709

It is not love of children that drives McDonald's Corp. to offer "Happy Meal" toys to kids. Instead, a simple marketing strategy drives these business giveaways. The corporation is successfully conditioning the defenseless minds of children, hooking them on its food—as if they were Pavlov's dogs. *This is an example of why we teach our kids to never accept gifts from strange clowns.*

710

When it comes to protecting our children, Uncle Sam would not be so frequently required to pick up the ball and run with it if so many negligent parents were not always fumbling it away.

711

We need liberals *and* conservatives—old-time conservatives, not authoritarian Tea Partiers—to balance the most promising ideas for the future with the most successful ideas from the past. It is regrettable that this breed of conservative no longer has a party.

712

Our Constitution was not divinely inspired or engraved in stone.

713

Sure, most of our revolutionary founders were conservative—*in the same way Jesus was* (i.e., only in the minds of delusional people).

714

History shows us that the Church has never taught us morality; rather, *we* have always taught the Church.

715

The nuttier that nuts get, the saner the rest of us appear—but if we meet them on middle ground, we all end up in the nuthouse.

716

Religious confession is a cheap way to wash away guilt, for it allows us to commit misdeeds with little lasting harm to our consciences. Such leniency with guilt leads to recidivism; *hence, the wronged should be the only ones granting absolution.*

717

The more you permit others—especially religious institutions—to direct your conscience, the more it will atrophy.

718

For families, it now takes two incomes to provide what one did four decades ago. Both parents must work these days, which leaves inadequate time for them to properly raise their children.

This has led to the fracturing of our family structures—and to emerging fault lines that have spread across society. Since the economic policies of the GOP were dominant throughout this period, we can see that Republican values are to blame for the disintegration of our family values. In other words, the GOP double-crossed us.

719

Blaming poor people for our economic problems is like yelling at a starving servant for stealing a missing apple pie—as a pudgy princeling watches, fingering apple filling off his fat face.

720

To make *The Adventures of Huckleberry Finn* less objectionable to some, a new version replaces the words "Injun" and "nigger" with "Indian" and "slave." If the liberals who prompt this strain of censorship were to peer into a mirror, they would see right-wing extremists roasting books around a bonfire.

721

There are no such things as bad words—only words that are used badly.

722

We can see the difference between Democrats and Republicans by examining their negotiation methods: Democrats primarily use reason while Republicans put guns to the heads of hostages.

723

Loyalty is a flawed concept: it encourages us to excuse conduct that we often should be condemning.

724

For 30 years, conservative Christians have successfully badgered Republican presidents into packing federal courts with activist judges who sanction "God's" will. It is not Islamic sharia law that we must fear, but Christian fundamentalist law—for it has already infected many of our highest courts.

725

President Obama directs the actions of Tea Partiers: whatever he supports, they oppose. In essence, he defines who they are.

726

Just hours ago, Congresswoman Gabrielle Giffords was shot in the head. In last year's campaign cycle, Sarah Palin had put her on a "target list." *Unless this is but a coincidence*, we should hold Palin accountable for instigating an attempted assassination.

727

This book will influence people. And just as I will gladly take a share of the credit if it inspires somebody to do good, *I must also take a share of the blame if it inspires somebody to do evil* (and it does not matter if this individual was already unhinged, for we know that psychopaths are within every audience). All media figures must accept this responsibility; if they do not, there will always be inadequate self-regulation of incendiary rhetoric—and their words will too frequently kill.

728

Yes, there are extremists on both ends of the political spectrum— but the ones on the right pack guns while the ones on the left pack weed pipes.

729

If you had a crazy neighbor, would you object to me repetitively speaking to him about you, spouting inflammatory statements couched in suggestively violent language?

730

It is acceptable for political and media personalities to criticize the opinions of anybody. On the other hand, it is *never* acceptable to endorse "Second Amendment remedies," rallying supporters to "reload" and "take out" all the "enemies" who are "targeted" for being "anti-American."

731

While we bash Muslims for not repudiating Islamic figures who use rabble-rousing language, many conservatives are defending right-wing media commentators who use similar language—*even though everybody's fringe elements are equally impressionable.*

732

Why have we banned marijuana, but not semi-automatic handguns with high-capacity clips?

733

Owning a gun is seldom about self-defense; instead, it is almost always about exerting power over others.

734

America is an addict that is refusing to address its issues. It will inevitably make necessary changes after it hits rock bottom—but do we really want to go there?

735

When someone hates our government, they hate you and me.

736

I guess a semi-automatic handgun with a high-capacity clip would come in handy when hunting packs of killer rabbits for dinner.

737

Until voted into office, our armed rebels should stick to shooter video games—and leave the running of our country to the adults.

738

Never allow somebody to pressure or shame you into not using our courts. They belong to all of us, not just the aristocrats.

739

In the summer of 2010, right-wing radio host Joyce Kaufman stated, "If ballots don't work, bullets will." Months later, Rep. Allen West, a newly elected Tea Partier, nearly hired her as his chief of staff. West had won notoriety during his campaign by telling angry supporters to make his opponent "scared to come out of his house." Kaufman and West illustrate hawks of a feather flocking together— but the caws of this sizable, predatory flock are not like the pleasant twitters of most other American birds.

740

Some people would enjoy the hobby of collecting and setting off cherry bombs; however, for the safety of society, we do not let them practice it. Similarly, though many gun nuts may enjoy the hobby of collecting and shooting handguns, their amusement can never outweigh the harm caused by the proliferation of their "toys" — *so we should ban handguns*. And if their owners need a substitute hobby, they can take up stamp collecting.

741

Comparing the violent rhetoric of right-wingers to that of left-wingers is like comparing *The Godfather* to *The Road Runner Show*.

742

Our society is like a Jenga tower: the wooden blocks are public resources and the players are plutocrats. In the beginning, the tower is evenly arranged and sturdy, with the upper, middle, and lower "levels" getting equal blocks. One by one, however, players pull them out of the middle and bottom, depositing them atop all others. The upper level rises ever higher, majestically, as the others grow weak and unstable. Predictably, the tower collapses —and despite the fact that one person does win, the game ends for everybody.

743

From the future, Big Brother now speaks through the mouth of Fox *Propaganda*.

744

Before people deny being liberals, they should at least take some time to look up the definition of this political label that they find so distasteful. What they discover might surprise them.

745

Though most people like much of the liberal platform, they still detest all labels that are even remotely associated with it (e.g., progressive, leftist, socialist, communist). It has always been easier for right-wingers to defame names rather than policies.

746

Left-wing pundits did not write the assessment that "lone wolves and small terrorist cells embracing violent rightwing extremist ideology are the most dangerous domestic terrorism threat in the United States." Rather, it was the terrorism experts within the Department of Homeland Security that came to this conclusion.

747

After correctly claiming that books influence people, right-wing pundits went on to insist that inflammatory rhetoric on conservative radio and television programs *has no effect on disturbed individuals*. Then—when critics attempted to address this rhetoric—the pundits censured the conversations, asserting that such discussions were dangerous and reprehensible. Once again, the party of personal responsibility is shirking all blame: even though Republicans take credit for fueling right-wing enthusiasm—everyone else is guilty of igniting right-wing extremism.

748

Power wheelchairs are great for home defense: I own two, and no one has ever robbed or assaulted me in my house. Sadly, the press refuses to report the many stories of individuals deterring criminals by keeping wheelchairs in their homes. I know you may never buy my claim, but you should—*considering that most of us have bought similar snake oil for years from gun lobbyists.*

749

It would be nice if we tape delayed every political interview so that broadcasters could bleep out all of the *truth* malfunctions.

750

Respect for other cultures should never sway us to condone their injustices. First, *it is* our business because the dividing line that separates cultures is arbitrary: does it fall beyond one's state, country, continent, *planet*—or front doorstep? And second, no culture's ethical code is inherently superior—which means that we must, as always, judge according to our own conscience.

751

The czar of the GOP, Rush Limbaugh, stated, "Civility is the new censorship." Even if you are correct, Rush, there is no need to whine about it—unless your livelihood is built on *in*civility.

752

By privatizing Social Security, we will be trading a dependable *insurance* plan for yet another retirement account. So, how have your other savings plans panned out—and could they sustain you through life if you became permanently disabled tomorrow?

753

The GOP apparently *does* have a plan for dealing with many of our social problems: gather everyone who is broke, uneducated, or mentally ill into taverns, get them all shitfaced—*and hand out semi-automatic handguns with high-capacity clips.*

754

If you object to the "individual mandate" within the Affordable Care Act, I would agree to you receiving an exemption—on one condition: you must sign a contract stating that you will *never* accept *any* health care services during your *entire* life unless you pay for them yourself in full *without recourse to bankruptcy.*

755

Just one week after the attempted assassination of Rep. Giffords, Daily Kos had Public Policy Polling ask people, "Do you think violence against the current American government is justified?" With Tea Partiers, 13% said yes (only 4% of all others answered likewise). Put bluntly, *one of every eight Tea Partiers supports this brand of domestic terrorism*. Knowing that we can judge a group by the company it keeps—do we really want the Tea Party to dictate the governance of our nation?

756

Hemlock is "all natural"—but I would not recommend eating it.

757

Although our world is certain to have a day of reckoning, let us not rush it—for it will be very unpleasant for all civil folk.

758

I would rather be a socialist taxpayer than a capitalist slave.

759

"Uncertainty" is the latest catchword of Republicans. They tell us that we must eliminate specifically *business* uncertainty, and that the wellbeing of our economy is at stake. If this is not a lie, it is at best an exaggeration. Business and uncertainty go hand in hand, and if they did not—if entrepreneurs encountered no risks—we would all start a business. In truth, uncertainty helps capitalism by weeding out shortsighted, unadaptable entities. I just wish the GOP would put some effort into reducing the more numerous uncertainties that are facing individuals who are not wealthy enough to own a business.

760

We should give our aristocrats lots of certainty by promising to reinstate and lock in the steeper upper income tax rates and the stricter regulations that were in place before Reagan's war on the working class commenced—*and by resolutely keeping our word.*

761

They shot at a target with the initials of Rep. Debbie Wasserman Schultz; they hung an effigy of Rep. Frank Kratovil; they tarred and feathered an effigy of Rep. Alan Boyd; etc. So where do you think these right-wing simulations of violence against Democrats will lead us...?

762

John F. Kennedy, Medgar Evers, Martin Luther King Jr., Robert F. Kennedy, George R. Moscone, Harvey Milk, John Lennon, Alan Berg, Robert Smith Vance, Robert E. Robinson, James E. Davis, and Bill Gwatney. Now—having shown my quick list of liberal Americans who have died by the hands of assassins over the last 50 years—I wait for anybody to show me a list of conservatives who have met the same fate. *I bet that my list will always be much longer.*

763

Given that we have a minimum age requirement to become the president of our country—would it not be equally wise to have a maximum?

764

In the 11 days since the shooting of Rep. Giffords, she has made miraculous progress with her recovery. Nevertheless, there are

Republicans who are already demanding that she surrender her congressional seat. This is unfair: even when Giffords was in a medically induced coma, she was no less willing and able to *sincerely* serve America than the majority of her GOP colleagues are on a healthy day.

765

Bear in mind that our founders granted us the right to amend *any* section of our Constitution—even the anachronistic Second Amendment.

766

Conservative Christianity teaches obedience to authority without question, and right-wing politicians rely on blind obedience. Hence, they formed a union 30 years ago: a match made in hell.

767

While serving as President Reagan's budget director from 1981 to 1985, David Stockman instituted Reaganomics—*and has decried it as a failure ever since*. In a 2010 op-ed article, Stockman wrote that our "debt explosion has resulted not from big spending by the Democrats, but instead the Republican Party's embrace, about three decades ago, of the insidious doctrine that deficits don't matter if they result from tax cuts." If Dr. Frankenstein tells us that his creation is a monster, we should not pause to debate his reasoning as it continues to ravage our countryside.

768

The true objective of Reaganomics—other than to further enrich our aristocrats—was to slash tax revenues, *thereby necessitating matching spending cuts*. David Stockman, the coordinator of this "starve the beast" scheme, recently delivered his verdict on it:

"The lesson of the last 25 years is that it doesn't work." With our natural inclination to avoid pain, we let the beast binge on debt (i.e., junk food) instead of putting it on a diet. So, as Stockman put it, "We have now created so much national debt, and such large permanent deficits that we're going to have to do some very difficult and painful things to close the gap, or we're going to destroy the economy, and render the federal government insolvent." In other words, we must soon feed the beast some healthier food by increasing our tax revenues—or many of us will starve along with it. By Stockman's calculation, "we're going to be in the tax-raising business for the next decade."

769

Easy credit encourages us to purchase things that we generally would not if we were using just our hard-earned money. For example, it is unlikely that we would have bought Dubya's two costly wars if we were unable to totally cover them with *trillions* of dollars of debt. As long as we can pay for public programs without digging into our pockets, we will have little incentive to cut anything. Regrettably, Reagan did not consider this before he launched the GOP's 30-year campaign to "starve the beast." In a land of credit, only financial fools and frauds cut revenues *before* expenses.

770

Do tax cuts "starve the beast"—or do they raise revenues? The GOP needs to make up its mind.

771

My Green Bay Packers are returning to the Super Bowl! Yes, I am a sports fan and I am proud to be one, for it has made me both a happier person and a wiser patriot. As a fan, I have learned that I sound like an imbecile if I claim my team is number one when they obviously are not; that my team can move from the top of the league to the bottom, and vice versa, very rapidly; that I am no less of a fan when I question my team's decisions; and that every team has equally dedicated fans who also boast about exceptionalism. Now I will end this rumination by shouting, "GO PACK GO!"

772

You can hear echoes from our slavery past in the words of the fear mongers who ceaselessly fight all our efforts to increase the minimum wage.

773

Conservatives prefer established customs and values, and tend to resist change. If the past has treated one well, it makes sense to adopt such a mindset; otherwise, it is masochistic to do so.

774

Sarah Palin recently babbled about the Soviet's "race to space": "Yeah, they won, but they also incurred so much debt at the time that it led to the inevitable collapse of the Soviet Union." In fact, *military* spending ruined the Soviet economy, just as it is ruining ours. *Sarah, since you do not even dimly know the past, you are not qualified to lead us into the future.*

775

Two weeks ago, Rep. Michele Bachmann, cofounder of the House Tea Party Caucus, delivered a speech in Iowa. She praised early American immigrants by stating, "It didn't matter the color of their skin.... Once you got here, we were all the same!" As for slavery, she noted that our founders "worked tirelessly until slavery was no more in the United States." *Congratulations, Michele—Glenn Beck University now wants to grant you a history professorship!*

776

"I don't believe in evolution" translates into "I have never really studied evolution, nor do I wish to do so."

777

Privatization widens all doors for people of greed.

778

The sooner we treat our children like adults, the sooner they will behave like adults.

779

For the clergy, the dubious promise of a heavenly afterlife is the cheapest, yet most potent currency for buying the obedience of the masses.

780

While humans domesticated the world, the world domesticated humans.

781

The only votes that are capable of doing a democracy justice are those that are based on empathy.

782

American slaveholders failed to sell capitalism to their slaves: by just awarding a few of them token wealth, the owners could have then convincingly lied about how *anybody* can prosper with enough hard work.

783

Corporate America would pounce on any opportunity to employ slaves; the massive outsourcing of jobs to overseas sweatshops proves this.

784

If China backed a vicious dictatorship in America because it was politically and economically friendly, how would most of us feel about China's government? If you are unsure, simply ask some Egyptians or Tunisians how they feel about ours.

785

A message to Washington and corporate America: there is no such thing as an acceptable dictatorship.

786

Once we invest our Social Security funds in the stock market, we will never own corporations: they will own us. We will concede whatever they demand—for our prosperity will hinge on theirs.

787

Capitalists have issues with legitimate democracies because they breed uncertainty. Consequently, America prefers a variation on this style of government: *a democracy of one*. We have befriended dozens of such iron-fisted, "democratic" regimes over the years.

788

The Tea Party is blackballing every Republican that supports *any* Democratic initiative. It accepts no compromises or differences of opinion. Put plainly, it is just a gang of tyrants.

789

One month after he helped ram an extension of Bush's tax cuts down our throats, House Speaker John Boehner declared, "We're broke." It would have been nice for him to tell us this *before* we gave away billions of dollars of America's tax revenues to filthy rich hoarders.

790

The predominantly peaceful demonstrations for democracy in Egypt have moved the world. Glenn Beck, though, is saying that the uprising "is being orchestrated by the Marxist communists." *And so right-wingers begin their time-honored magic trick of turning pro-democracy heroes into leftist villains.*

791

Until God registers to vote, he should shut the hell up.

792

Americans do not mind bullies—as long as they work for us.

793

We do not know whether the pro-democracy activists in Egypt will be victorious, but we should give them a chance—just as France did with our founders over two centuries ago.

794

The chief defense mechanism of the GOP is *right-wing projection*. This involves publicly transferring the party's antisocial actions, thoughts, and desires to Democrats (in other words, the GOP is guilty of nearly everything it accuses others of doing.)

795

If you want to be a better Christian, follow Jesus—not God.

796

Internet piracy hurts sales no more than library lending does.

797

We should subject corporations to the same invasive means tests that humans must endure to receive public assistance.

798

America already has black markets for guns: we call them gun shows.

799

Since the GOP is so successful at distracting us with fabricated issues, most conservatives are unaware of the real threats to our security—the Four Horsemen of the Corporations: War, Slavery, Poverty, and Pollution.

800

A new poll by VTsIOM showed that 32% of Russians believe the sun orbits the earth. Before we deride their ignorance, however, we must see if religion induced it. If so, we can only praise them —for it is politically incorrect to mock pious self-delusion.

801

For our aristocracy, the American Dream is but a nightmare of unwelcomed competition.

802

More than half of all Americans watched at least some portion of this year's Super Bowl, in which my Green Bay Packers held on to beat the Pittsburgh Steelers in a nail-biting struggle—*and not one person needed to die for the cause.* Perhaps we can learn to feed our hunger for nationalistic conquest with less destructive fare, such as what we get through sports. (We must be wary, though, for our leaders will still exploit our competitiveness to move us from our athletic fields to their battlefields.)

803

My disease has stolen nearly every muscle in my body, but it has fortunately left me those that are most vital for promoting both health and prosperity: the facial muscles that form my smile.

804

We should start collecting happiness instead of thingamajigs and doodads—which really only serve to make their sellers happy.

805

It is possible that the Muslim Brotherhood will not obstruct Egypt's efforts to install an authentic democracy. After all, our Christian fundamentalists have not hijacked *our* democracy—yet. This does raise a question, however: are Egyptians likewise fretting over our religious fanatics and the threat they pose to America?

806

The primary cause for the recent outbreak of civil unrest in the Arab world is not a political one, but economic: the income gap between the filthy rich and everyone else has grown too huge for the have-nots to accept. And as capitalists everywhere continue to pillage while enforcing austerity measures, *we all move closer to joining the Arab uprisings*. Can you hear Marx's ghost laughing?

807

Our Tea Partiers look exactly like the Egyptian protestors; more specifically, *the right-wing, pro-Mubarak thugs*.

808

The Electoral College is undemocratic; we must abolish it. With the way it funnels most campaign resources into swing states, it marginalizes the voters from other areas: a Democratic voter in Utah and a Republican voter in Hawaii are not equal to the ones in Florida. Also, it underhandedly tosses the minority votes of every state in a national tally. *The Electoral College produces voter inequality by design, thereby corrupting the very heart of America's democracy.*

809

Now that our aristocrats are wolfing down all of the meat in our economy, they are pushing us to fight like dogs for fallen table scraps. We should be snarling at our "masters," not each other.

810

Contrary to what our warlords wish us to believe, humans are not naturally violent; rather, they are naturally *trainable*. In other words, we have loyally served through history as Rottweilers for a never-ending lineup of predatory rulers (i.e., handlers).

811

Capitalism is merely a manipulated system for redistributing all wealth to the aristocracy—*along with our blessings*.

812

Most of us are good people—*as long as we do not yield our will to immoral leaders.* They are the ones who coax us into doing ugly deeds for their gains, so we must spurn them. By following our own untampered consciences, we will most often be decent.

813

"Swearing on the Bible" is the feeblest form of truth serum.

814

In this economic crisis, many of us have labored harder to cover for laid-off employees. These workloads will now become the norm—for capitalists exploit *every* sacrifice.

815

If you are a unionized teacher who does not support firing inept co-workers, you love your union—*not* students. In essence, you are deliberately placing their lives in the hands of incompetent brain surgeons. Anybody who "loves" our students in this way will get such love requited accordingly.

816

We should be ashamed that we are placing students in school lotteries to choose the privileged few who will receive a quality education. Due to our failure to maintain enough good schools, *we are now playing Russian roulette with children.* For this disgrace, we shall all be damned in the end.

817

A winner without honor is still a loser.

818

Self-delusion entails the swallowing of lies, those of others as well as one's own. Over time, one fosters a taste for such lies— and they become ever easier to ingest *or issue*. And thus, the more religious one is (i.e., self-deluded), the more comfortable one frequently ends up being with dishonesty.

819

Deception is the prime fertilizer of religions.

820

Voter fraud normally involves a person tricking others into not casting their ballots—not a person casting *extra* ballots. Hence, the opportunities for fraud will only increase if we add hoops for people to jump through in order to vote: each one complicates the process, making a trickster's job simpler.

821

There is a surefire way to eliminate all voter fraud: eliminate all voting. (Note to right-wingers: I'm just being facetious, so please don't seriously give any consideration to this idea. Oops, too late....)

822

It is better to have women degrade me by seeing me as a piece of meat than it is to have them see me as a *degraded* piece of meat.

823

I maneuver my power wheelchair by sipping and puffing into a straw, and I am not good with crowds. Nevertheless, today I went to the Wisconsin State Capitol to join the protest against

Governor Scott Walker's union busting bill. Roughly 65,000 like-minded persons were there. No harm came to me; the protestors were commendably peaceful—as they have been since the start, four days ago. Fox *Propaganda*, though, keeps portraying many of them as leftist rioters bent on violence. Now I have witnessed Fox's deceits first hand, confirming that we cannot trust *anything* it reports.

824

Our plutocrats have a plan to eradicate unemployment: first, we must all agree to work for free....

825

Condemn the religion—not its followers (i.e., victims).

826

To meet a *true* disciple of Jesus is a rare, moving experience.

827

The Tea Partier definition of democracy: "Shut up and do what I say!"

828

Because of Governor Walker's union busting bill, many teachers around Wisconsin are staging a sickout, closing schools. It is causing inconvenience, particularly to parents. Some are upset and want to force the teachers back to work. But this is unjust: nobody is ever obligated to clean our streets, protect our homes, teach our children, etc. If we cannot compel corporations to do as we bid, why do we think that we can compel individuals? They must receive the same free market rights that businesses enjoy. When we want goods or services from them, we bargain; we should do no less with people—even if we are paying them with tax dollars.

829

Corporate America is using its contract killers within the media and government to murder its hated adversaries—labor unions. And if they die, we will lose our last credible means for keeping wages and benefits from plunging. Without them, corporations will unrestrainedly exploit America's oversupply of workers by coercing us to undercut one another in the job market, year after year.

830

Republicans receive their big donations from corporations while Democrats receive theirs from labor unions. Should these few unions perish, *the Democratic Party would not die*; rather, it would sell itself to corporate America, as the GOP has done. Though we would retain two parties, we would essentially wind up with a single-party system—a sham democracy run by corporations.

831

New Jersey Governor Chris Christie recently said, "I'm attacking the leadership of the union because they're greedy, and they're selfish, and they're self-interested." Given that this seems to be a description of the quintessential free market capitalist, why are Republicans harassing unions and their leaders? They are model Americans, having learned well from our corporate executives.

832

Yesterday, Governor Christie declared, "There can no longer be two classes of citizens: one that receives rich health and pension benefits, and all the rest who are left to pay for them." After many years of waging stealthy class warfare, our plutocrats are at last openly declaring hostilities against us. There is a bizarre twist, however: they now intend to fight public workers in the middle class with other workers *from the same class*. The GOP ringleaders are in effect yelling, "Let's you and him fight!"

833

I can see how white voters could be scared away from polling places by New Black Panthers. On the other hand, I can also see how black voters could be scared away from polling places by Tea Partiers. So, knowing that there are only a few New Black Panthers and *millions* of Tea Partiers, which gang poses a greater voter intimidation threat?

834

Ten years ago, I bought a mobile home. Even with my good credit scores and a down payment, the best rate I could find for a loan was 10.75%. Lenders say that these loans are risky; hence, I am paying tens of thousands of dollars extra. *This is the greatest factor that would cause me to default.* And if I did, these loan sharks—these self-fulfilling prophets—would accept no blame.

835

In general, we more readily give our trust to attractive people. This means that they seldom need to work as hard as others do to earn this trust. Consequently, who is more predisposed to deceive, a beauty or a beast?

836

From the beginning, our country has suffered from an anarchic cancer known as states' rights.

837

I live in a decent mobile home. I am not trailer trash. To avoid disturbing the county's finer folk, I had to place my home within a "park." Perhaps *I am* trailer trash. *This is how we ghettoize.*

838

As unsafe as nuclear power is, fossil fuels are worse because of their pervasive pollution. Radiation just sounds scarier.

839

You might be an *aspiring dictator* if you keep telling the public that you must once again exercise "emergency" powers.

840

Liberals are good at getting our forgiveness with an apology—and conservatives are good at getting our forgiveness with an excuse.

841

Republican politicians tend to believe that most Americans stand with them and Democratic politicians tend to believe that most Americans stand *against* them. Both parties are usually wrong, to our detriment.

842

We are far down the road to global ruin, and our plutocrats love the scenery too much to ever voluntarily change course. *We must force them to take a drastically different route.* Many of us do know the way, but unless we shout in unison, they will never hear us. The Tea Party cannot join in, for it is just a tool of the plutocrats. Perhaps the recent labor rallies that are spreading outward from

Wisconsin can lead to the thunderous unification of our voices. If so, we may yet have enough time to veer away from doomsday.

843

Behind all great leaders, there are throngs of ordinary citizens pushing them forward.

844

Obsess less over the bad things you have done and more over the good things you will do to make amends.

845

Many of the laws that are needed to discourage the misdeeds of exploitative capitalists are already on the books, but are not being enforced. This suggests an experiment: if the police ever stop you, point out that they can selectively enforce laws—*and see if it helps.*

846

Two years ago, oil profiteers learned a lesson: to keep us from demanding renewables, they must jack up gasoline prices *slowly.*

847

Given that we do not like our elected representatives listening to lobbyists, *why do we keep listening to the very same hucksters?*

848

In 1973, *The Atlantic Monthly* quoted a scientist who articulated the pharmaceutical industry's thinking on the common practice of carrying out medical experiments on convicts: "Criminals in our penitentiaries are fine experimental material—and much cheaper than chimpanzees." To be fair to Big Pharma, it is not alone in treating humans inhumanely: all true capitalists will sell anyone for a buck. In their minds, we are merely disposable assets —no better than laboratory chimps.

849

If God had truly wanted to discourage homosexuality, he probably should not have placed the male prostate next to the rectal wall —creating a G-spot. He completely screwed up *that* design.

850

I will agree to grant corporations the status of personhood on the same day that we devise a way to incarcerate the bad ones.

851

When our partners go elsewhere for physical stimulation, why are we more distraught than when they go elsewhere for *mental* stimulation?

852

If you have numerous employment options, but none of them pays a living wage, you are still only slightly freer than a slave.

853

House Speaker John Boehner just shared his thoughts regarding unions for public workers, stating, "We've given them a machine gun and put it right at the heads of the local officials and they really have their hands tied." For this to be true, the unionists must be loading the machine gun with water and binding hands with wet spaghetti. *How else can one explain the fact that union workers in the public sector earn no more in total pay and benefits than their private sector counterparts do?* No matter how the GOP spins the situation, this is the single fact that counts.

854

Public unions negotiate contracts with government officials. *So do businesses.* Public unions give campaign donations to some of the same officials. Again, *so do businesses.* Public unions and businesses deal with our government in similar ways; thus, if it is inappropriate for government officials to bargain with public unions, *it is equally inappropriate to do so with businesses.*

855

I cannot guarantee that we will improve our public school systems by spending more money—but I can guarantee that we will worsen them by spending less.

856

Uncle Sam's underlying motivation to instigate military conflict has always been to enrich businesses—via seizures of resources and war profiteering. Our leaders never disclose this; instead, they use false pretenses to secure our support. Though it would be nice to hear the truth, it will not happen: if our president said, "To make companies like Halliburton, General Dynamics, Xe, Bechtel, and ExxonMobil more profitable, I want to invade a weak country in the Middle East," most of us would not sign on to the plan. Consequently, our leaders will keep censoring the reality that we go to war primarily for the sake of *corporate* America.

857

Our arms industry manufactures innumerable products that we have no need for—some of which not even the Pentagon wants. Still, Congress rarely eliminates any of these boondoggles: for each possible cut, there are politicians seeking reelection who will be in opposition, protecting the businesses and workers in a home district. Since such businesses are building little of value, we are in essence paying them billions of dollars for bridges to nowhere. We must either stop the flow of tax funds or compel the arms industry to retool so that it can provide our country some worthier products (e.g., schools, wind farms, high-speed rail systems—or bridges to *anywhere*).

858

Would you ever knowingly employ a severely paranoid man to guard your family, *giving him free use of your credit cards to procure* any *weapons that he longs for*? If not, why have we employed the Pentagon under the same arrangement to guard our country?

859

Conservatives are God-fearing—and liberals are Jesus-loving.

860

The true objective of our legal system is to enforce order. Any justice that we receive is simply a byproduct.

861

Poverty-stricken children are focusing on matters such as hunger and sickness—not on acing a test to make us proud. *These kids obviously do not have their priorities as straight as we do.*

862

This morning, I found an extra sock in my dresser. No one knows how it got there. None of our theories can explain it. We have no first-hand evidence that a natural agent was involved—and it is hard to believe that "chance" played some role. Clearly, God must have created this "well-designed" sock, planting it in the dresser. It is miraculous: *a sock has proved the existence of God!*

863

The BP oil spill is still a disaster site. The contamination keeps poisoning the people and wildlife. But there is no cause for us to be alarmed: since America has successfully forgotten the whole mess—*it no longer exists.*

864

It is easy for conservatives to be God-fearing. After all, they are afraid of just about everybody who is different.

865

Local control of education has a fatal defect: ignorance begets ignorance (i.e., when a community raises a generation that fails educationally, that generation goes on to instruct the following one in the same flawed way).

866

We could solve multiple problems in our society by having a high school diploma be the minimum prerequisite for sex. (Lest I get abstinence fans too excited, I must mention that enforcing such a policy would create even worse problems.)

867

It is usually less expensive to provide long-term care services in a community setting (i.e., in one's home) than it is to do so in an institution (i.e., in a nursing home). Furthermore, people are far happier in their own homes, living longer. And there's the rub:

we pass away faster in nursing homes, which makes them the most cost-effective option in the end. Maybe this explains the peculiar unwillingness of so many conservatives to move funding out of institutional care and into community-based care. *Unchecked fiscal conservatism will always lead to the indirect application of involuntary euthanasia.*

868

The sorriest aspect of losing a political campaign: even if in the end your side can rightfully say, "We told you so," almost none of the voters on the other side will ever learn from their mistake.

869

Although the best soldiers are the ones who follow orders with *minimal* independent thought, the best generals are never those who do likewise. Unfortunately, most of our generals are customarily promoted from the ranks of our best soldiers.

870

I truly hope that Hell exists: how else will anybody be able to suitably punish our aristocrats for their unholy exploitation of everyone and everything on earth?

871

Most nursing homes serve as death camps for our unwanted.

872

The newest GOP governors are seizing dictatorial powers in their states; selling public assets at fire-sale prices to businesses; cutting and privatizing vital services; hiking up taxes and fees on lower- and middle-class citizens; and handing over all the cash saved and raised from these acts to the wealthy. *This is a taste of how a Tea Party-backed president will run our country.*

873

The more I examine the actions of those who claim to be divinely guided, the more I am convinced that God is either an idiot or a big practical joker.

874

If a person wraps an arm around you, insisting you are a friend, and then slides a knife into your back—you can be certain that that person never really was your friend. Remember this the next time a program slasher from the GOP tries to win you over.

875

The GOP now champions only *capitalist* causes. If some happen to match those of traditional conservatives, it is a coincidence.

876

We are jobless and hungry, but Tea Partiers are rushing to help: they are legislating morality so that we can suffer righteously.

877

Republicans condemn everyone who violates a contract—unless it is just an agreement made with workers, which is ungodly and un-American.

878

The danger posed by Fox *Propaganda* is rising: even the leaders of the GOP are now drinking its Kool-Aid.

879

If welfare does have a disincentive effect on worker productivity —as conservatives claim—why do we then assume that corporate welfare has the opposite effect on *business* productivity?

880

It is true that businesses create jobs—but we laborers produce and buy their goods and services. Business owners rely on us as much as we rely on them, and so they deserve the same respect that they are giving us. *Put differently, we should be kicking their asses rather than kissing them.*

881

The federal budget requires liposuction, but none of our "surgeons" is targeting the fat in the torso. Democrats are aiming for the hands, Republicans are aiming for the feet, and Tea Partiers are aiming for all of the internal organs—particularly the brain.

882

Sooner or later, our workers will lead a revolution: if sooner, it can be peaceful; if later, it will surely be violent.

883

I love Wisconsin—but I am an American, not a Wisconsinite. As Americans, we must stop letting plutocrats divide and conquer us state by state. We are stronger as one team instead of fifty.

884

There is something more controlling than a federal government: federal, state, county, and local governments ganged together.

Even when one of them does not tread on us commoners, the next usually does. Hence, we need to bring them all to heel.

885

Ronald Reagan popularized the GOP's eleventh commandment: "Thou shalt not speak ill of any fellow Republican." To this, I would like to attach a twelfth commandment: "Thou shalt not put the interests of any political party before those of America." More than any other rule, this one would damn the GOP to hell.

886

Attempting to civilize warfare is like trying to transform angry alcoholics into social drinkers: no matter how many conventions the alcoholics agree to abide by to regulate their conduct, once the booze begins to flow, they will always disregard moderation.

887

Like you, the Koch brothers each have one vote. But in addition, they have billions of dollars that they are effectively using to sway countless other voters. *How much cash do you have to do the same?* We are too poor to buy our share of democracy.

888

If only for our own good, we must strive to outlaw every form of sweatshop labor within the global market: either we will coerce businesses to raise wages in developing countries—or our wages will steadily fall to match theirs.

889

The more I observe minimum-wage laborers at work, the more shame I feel. Most of them work very hard—and they deserve at least *living* wages. If we cannot afford such pay, it is further proof that capitalism is a broken system in need of an overhaul.

890

Meditation is not an arcane skill that only monks can do. It is easy: go to a serene place, sit comfortably, and free your mind to wander. It will then find what you truly need.

891

For the most part, the aristocracy has successfully separated us from our mass media outlets, governmental bodies, and courts. And so it is now ramping up its efforts to take out our last few unions: if they perish, we will be completely isolated, for the aristocracy will have finally severed our last remaining links to one another.

892

There are major differences between the recent pro-union rallies and those of the Tea Party: specifically, the pro-union ones are much larger, they are receiving far less media coverage, and they are fighting authentic threats (e.g., not imaginary death panels).

893

When setting your expectations regarding events that you have no control over, be conservative: at worst, your expectations will be met; at best, you will be pleasantly surprised.

894

Self-confidence is the main trait that separates average persons who succeed from average persons who fail. (By the way, most of us are average.)

895

If ignoramuses will agree to keep their feeble minds out of serious public debates, I will agree to keep my feeble body out of their professional wrestling rings.

896

When businesses make and revise their plans, they examine *future* costs and benefits: *past amounts spent or earned are irrelevant.* One should follow this practice when making and revising *life* plans. For example, never sink additional effort into a lost cause—no matter how much one has already invested in it.

897

Statistics compiled by the nonpartisan Tax Foundation prove that red states are generally the worst welfare queens. By comparing the federal monies that each state receives to the federal taxes it pays, we learn that the biggest beneficiaries are usually red states. If their conservative voters really wish to balance the federal budget, they should lead by example: they can give back some of their welfare or pay their fair share with higher taxes.

898

Republicans still do not understand that an ounce of prevention is worth a pound of cure. They keep gutting the programs that help people be law-abiding citizens (e.g., mental health care, substance abuse treatment, education, welfare, community development) while paying tens of billions of dollars each year to incarcerate millions. How is this fiscally conservative?

899

Between the womb and a prison, the GOP has no interest in us.

900

If the South had won the Civil War, the world would now have two Mexicos.

901

If you take Archie Bunker and remove his few endearing qualities —you end up with a Tea Partier.

902

The biggest fools are the fools who keep on forgetting that they are fools.

903

In Japan and the Gulf of Mexico, we have received object lessons on the dangers of nuclear power and oil. *I wonder what happens in a windmill or solar panel disaster.*

904

Our military is torturing the suspected WikiLeaks whistleblower, Army Pfc. Bradley Manning, within a Marine Corps brig—even though he is a truer patriot than Sen. John McCain now pretends to be.

905

Republicans love fetuses. Democrats love babies.

906

If you do not care about the concerns of others, you must never count on them to care about yours.

907

Some people believe that members of an ethnic minority cannot be racists. If this is correct, what term should we use for the white minority citizens of South Africa who supported apartheid?

908

Our government is broken because we the people are broken. This should not unduly alarm us, however, for the fix is clear-cut: we just need to come together. Once reunited, our government will again be of the people, by the people, and for the people. *We are our government.*

909

Most registered Republicans are not mean persons: they merely need some regular visits from Ebenezer's ghosts.

910

To translate GOP statements, find a good book of antonyms.

911

Though Tea Partiers hate corporate bailouts, they love corporate incentives, such as tax breaks and subsidies. This is as absurd as hating larceny while loving thievery.

912

As Americans rally to defend the collective bargaining rights of public workers, unionists should examine the feelings that this latest loss of liberty has aroused. They are the same ones that women feel when we pay them less than we do men; that black people feel when we imprison them for minor offenses; that

Mexicans feel when we exploit them and then cast them aside; that homosexuals feel when we forbid them to marry the ones they love; that veterans feel when we ignore their needs after a war; that students feel when we deny them a decent education; that disabled people feel when we force them to live in nursing homes; that Muslims feel when we demonize them; that senior citizens feel when we abandon them to poverty; and that the uninsured feel when we refuse to heal them. We do not need to agree with everybody's opinions—*but we must all agree that we can no longer accept any of the actions that cause such feelings*. We must unite to protect *everybody's* rights.

913

A libertarian is no more independent from society than a heart is from its body.

914

If we did close our borders to all immigrants, how long would it be before America was weakened from cultural inbreeding?

915

Is your life wonderful or horrible? Ultimately, there is only one factor that defines the quality of your life: the way you choose to look at it. Nothing else matters.

916

Though Obama is a better president than *any* Republican could be, he is not the great president we need to rescue our country. We must find someone who will always do the right thing rather than the politically expedient thing. Someone who will trust in Main Street rather than Wall Street. Someone who will never concede.

917

When the Democratic Party gives you a lemon, it is still sweeter than the GOP's trickle-down "lemonade."

918

One is not ready to be married until one is ready to be single.

919

It is okay to make mistakes—but it is not okay to repeat them.

920

A recent survey by *Newsweek* revealed that 38% of Americans are incapable of passing the official citizenship test. Given that these individuals cannot meet this minimum standard, should we not be *de*naturalizing them? Perhaps immigrants are not our biggest problem.

921

Anybody who is too romantic to ask for a prenuptial agreement is also too irresponsible to be married. Simply consider that no husband- or wife-to-be ever expects a divorce (or an untimely death).

922

Good health is bad business for Big Pharma.

923

Lower voter turnout most often favors Republicans, so they try to make it harder for us to vote while Democrats try to make it easier.

Knowing that voter participation is the lifeblood of a democracy, which party's efforts should we decry as treason?

924

Al-Qaeda killed roughly 3000 innocent people on 9/11. Afterwards, America killed more than 100,000 innocent people in Iraq. Using an unprejudiced calculation, our crime was well over 30 times worse.

925

Jesus was a lover and Muhammad was a fighter—and their teachings reflect their natures. Although violent persons can pervert the words of the New Testament (or any other religious documents) to validate their evil actions, no distortion is necessary with the Qur'an. In fact, *peaceful* Muslims are the ones who must perform textual gymnastics to rationalize *non*violence.

926

An overwhelming majority of America's prison conversions are to Islam. This raises an apropos question: how is this religion so successfully whetting the appetites of our convicts? The answer likely lies in the battlefields that birthed the Qur'an.

927

What do you get when you take a charitable religious organization like the Salvation Army and discard the religious baggage? You get an even better organization, like the Red Cross.

928

Conservatives hate change. Consequently, when there is a crisis that reveals a need for change, they feel threatened. Their way of handling such a threat is always the same: quash all related dialogue by indignantly refusing to "politicize" the unfortunate situation—and then wait until we develop amnesia about it.

929

I predict that Islam will someday become the adopted religion of the Klingon warrior caste.

930

When buying a used home or vehicle, be wary: you are most often paying to acquire someone else's headache.

931

The real obstacle to the public's acceptance of evolution is not the existence of "gaps" within the fossil record; instead, it is the existence of gaps within the knowledge of our uneducated.

932

House Budget Committee Chairman Paul Ryan wrote the GOP's budget plan that kills Medicare and guts Medicaid, primarily to finance huge tax cuts for the wealthy. Many pundits are calling the plan courageous. I guess this is fair—if one believes a bully is courageous for announcing his intention to mug children, the elderly, the disabled, and the poor.

933

The 400 richest Americans own more wealth than the bottom 50% of our population (150 million people) *combined*. As Warren Buffett—one of the über-wealthy—stated, "There's class warfare, all right, but it's my class, the rich class, that's making war, and we're winning." Our government must intervene to rescue us from these economic warriors. To that end, I call on Paul Ryan to do something *genuinely* courageous: raise your masters' taxes!

934

I have known every form of discrimination—for I am disabled.

935

The disabled are nondiscriminatory: *everybody will someday join their ranks*. Hence, if only for self-interest, we should all fight for disabled rights.

936

If you fit too neatly into a defined school of thought, you have probably not been thinking enough.

937

I will condemn abortion on the day that most pro-lifers condemn war and state-sanctioned executions.

938

Reality TV and "monkey see, monkey do" produce an unstable brew.

939

The truth is no longer the truth: it is whatever Rupert Murdoch and the Koch brothers say it is. The two gravest threats to our democracy, Fox *Propaganda* and the Citizens United decision, have given them the ability to control or influence much of our news coverage and campaign advertisements, our key conduits for political information. By directing what people learn, these power-hungry billionaires are directing everyone's perception of truth—and thereby how we vote. Put simply, *they are hijacking our country.*

940

Through my teens, I trusted Republicans when they taught me that every famous liberal was corrupt. Then I grew disillusioned with the GOP and eventually realized that most of these liberals were in reality great Americans. My mentors had demonized them to suppress their ideology. Likewise, God taught me in my youth that Lucifer was corrupt. So when I recently grew disillusioned with God, I began to wonder....

941

Nearly half of all Americans pay no federal income tax, and I am one of them. Most of us have valid justification for not paying this tax: we are genuinely broke. Nonetheless, we *do* have skin in the game since we are still paying relatively big portions of our meager incomes for fees and taxes (e.g., FICA, state, local, sales, property). We cannot give much more than we are already handing over.

942

Among those that are paying no federal income tax are many wealthy corporations and individuals, like General Electric and John Paulson. Though they both just earned billions of dollars, they contributed less than a cent. *With an effective tax rate of 0%, these "job creators" should have already eliminated all unemployment.*

943

Tax expert David C. Johnston wrote that in 2007, our 400 highest income tax payers on average earned $345 million and paid a rate of about 17% for income and payroll taxes. Meanwhile, a median-wage, single worker earned $26,000 and shelled out more than 23% of this amount for the same batch of taxes. *Our once progressive tax system is now clearly regressive*—and the GOP does not want us to notice: through most of Dubya's presidency, such information concerning the top 400 taxpayers was a state secret.

944

Asking a Catholic priest for marriage advice is as nonsensical as asking a lifelong vegetarian for tips on making a great steak.

945

My thought for Good Friday: every time we support a state-sanctioned execution, we recrucify Jesus.

946

My thought for Easter: every time we support social justice, we resurrect Jesus.

947

Ayn Rand, the goddess of free market capitalists, was an atheist who condemned Christianity, calling it "the best kindergarten of communism possible." She also stated, "Faith is the worst curse of mankind, as the exact antithesis and enemy of thought." *When Christians espouse the cause of free markets, they are in effect forsaking Jesus for Rand.* So, what does God think of that?

948

Ayn Rand is giving atheists a bad name—for she was actually an antichrist. Atheists only deny the existence of deities. Rand, on the other hand, *overtly despised the teachings of Jesus.* And she is not the sole antichrist living among us: every true free market capitalist is one, though most are still hiding in their gilded closets.

949

Communism mirrors Christianity as capitalism mirrors Satanism.

950

Before the Revolutionary War, our aristocrats wanted the British army to protect them from the French and Indians. Once the army had done so, Britain tried to recoup some of the cost by levying minor taxes on the American colonies. As our greedy aristocrats did not want to pay their fair share, they hired thugs to incite riots. Thus, the poor—who were mostly unaffected by the taxes—became the ignorant pawns of the aristocrats, fighting for their cause at places like Boston Harbor. *And now we see how history is repeating itself with a certain manipulated party.*

951

Be wary when negotiating with anti-abortionists, for they do not deal in good faith (e.g., if you yield the final trimester, they will always attempt to sneak away with the full nine months).

952

Conservative Christians are trying to form a big government that imitates the intrusive behaviors of their own big religion.

953

We have the best constitution that our plutocrats will permit us to have (i.e., though there are amendments that would get strong majority support from the public, Congress will never even start the process for ratifying any of them).

954

I do not mind paying a federal gas tax of 18.4 cents per gallon —
but I do object to paying a vastly larger cut to Wall Street.

955

Republicans are like Neanderthals: they habitually use clubs in
place of scalpels when performing surgery on delicate problems.

956

Yesterday, an elite team of Navy SEALs killed Osama bin Laden
in his comfortable home within an upscale Pakistani city. In other
words, we did with a small counter-terrorism unit what we failed
to do with a large military force. This should teach us to stop
bringing WMDs to a gunfight.

957

We have killed bin Laden; however, before we declare victory,
we must factor in his stated objective of "bleeding America to
the point of bankruptcy" by making our generals race around
after al-Qaeda, causing "America to suffer human, economic, and
political losses without their achieving for it anything of note."
The best that we can sincerely claim with his death is a draw.

958

The GOP is determined to pass a constitutional amendment that
would call for a two-thirds vote in both the House and Senate to
raise taxes. The true aim of the GOP is to shield the aristocracy's
finances from our government. As an alternate plan, we should
pass an amendment that would call for a two-thirds vote *to cut*
taxes: this would shield *our government's finances* from the greedy
aristocracy.

959

Women equal men in sluttishness, but far surpass them in the ability to feign chastity.

960

International corporations are not actually working to transform Third World countries into likenesses of America; instead, these corporations are doing just the reverse (i.e., they seek to weaken our workforce, making it subservient).

961

Wall Street plays zero-sum games with our investments: when a "bankster" wins a dollar, the rest of us lose one. So if you really want to blame someone for taking our financial wealth, do not go after your neighbors. They also lost. Only Wall Street and its pals won, and every dollar of their obscene winnings came out of *our* pockets.

962

By fully knowing your own self, all others become predictable.

963

On paper, the Christian rapture sounds like a great deal to many atheists (although it would sound even better if every person of *any* religious faith would tag along for the ride).

964

In a recent Senate hearing addressing Big Oil's billions of dollars in gratuitous tax subsidies, Chevron CEO John Watson regurgitated a pretty Republican talking point: "I don't think the American

people want shared sacrifice. I think they want shared prosperity."
Though this comment is valid, it is also irrelevant—for we have
not shared sacrifices or prosperity for years. Our aristocrats keep
giving us all of the former while they take all of the latter.

965

Be wary of borrowing and lending with acquaintances, for too
many of them will subconsciously keep crooked ledgers.

966

When you need help putting your problems in perspective, visit
a few ICU patients.

967

Until we all stop going bonkers over royal weddings, we will not
be mature enough to see that our aristocrats are truly no better
than we are *in any way*—other than in wealth.

968

Last Sunday, Republican bigwig Newt Gingrich denounced Paul
Ryan's scheme to fundamentally alter Medicare, calling it "radical"
and "too big a jump." Two days later, Newt asserted, "Any ad
which quotes what I said on Sunday is a falsehood." Newt has
given us another glimpse into the Orwellian world of the GOP,
where truth is falsehood—and YouTube does not apparently exist.

969

After bin Laden's death, Rush Limbaugh stated, "If he [President
Obama] was a shoe-in for reelection, Osama bin Laden would still
be alive today," suggesting that Obama's real motivation for ordering
the mission was to enhance his chances at the polls. Limbaugh's

statement plainly illustrates the core failing in the thought processes of capitalists: *they believe everybody acts solely for self-gain.*

970

Show me a frequent social drinker—and I will show you a person who is frequently in trouble.

971

Of all types of buildings, airport terminals are the most manic-depressive.

972

Right-wing comedians are as rare as right-wing humanitarians. Evidently, the act of authoritative moneygrubbers plundering the world does not translate very well into funny.

973

Nerds laugh at jocks for misspellings while jocks laugh at nerds for laughing about misspellings. This is also how Democrats and Republicans interact in Washington.

974

In one breath, right-wingers tell us that America is exceptional—and in the next, they tell us all the many things that America cannot do, despite the successes of other countries. Indeed, it often sounds like these naysayers are about to hyperventilate.

975

On Memorial Day, rather than visiting cemeteries, we should be reading accurate history books to learn about how and why our military members actually died. Then, when we pause to offer them thanks, we can also beg forgiveness for having permitted Uncle Sam to sacrifice their lives in so many avoidable wars of imperialism.

976

While you have no right to harm people, you also have no duty to help. But always remember, the more often you choose to neglect others, the more often others will choose to neglect you.

977

Alan Greenspan spoke out today: "The fact that I am in favor of going back to the Clinton tax structure is merely an indication of how scared I am about ... this debt problem ... and its order of magnitude." Since America's long-standing "small government, free market economist" is this scared, *we should be listening*.

978

The surest way for us to transform nonviolent drug offenders into hardened criminals is to lock them all together in prisons.

979

If our criminal justice system is truly fair, why do good people most often feel anxious instead of safe around police officers?

980

Yesterday, Congress extended the Patriot Act—the mother of all big government intrusions. It passed largely on the strength of Republican votes. So why did most Tea Partiers not protest this continuing violation of our Constitution? Maybe they were still too "busy" trying to invalidate Obama's birth certificate.

981

Without broad community support, today's unwanted babies tend to become tomorrow's unwanted adults.

982

What everyone really needs are neighborhood churches—minus all of the religious distractions.

983

Regarding our terrorism security, if we are not willing and able to guard *every* public area, we might as well guard none of them.

984

The United States Conference of Catholic Bishops just released a study regarding the sexual abuse of minors by priests. Catholic bishops, organizations, and foundations financed nearly all of the research. As if trying to protect the church, the report noted that "priest-abusers were not 'pedophile priests'" because only "22 percent of victims were age ten and under." The persons involved with this whitewashing should pray that their religious beliefs are in error—or else they will all soon burn in Hell.

985

By insisting that gay couples be as good as the typical straight couple is at parenting, one is setting an extremely low bar.

986

Though legalization of same-sex marriage cannot lead to people marrying objects, animals, or children—for they can never give consent—it could lead to the acceptance of polygamy. I see no problem with this: if more than two persons wish to share their marital "bliss" with one another, it is none of our business.

987

Sarah Palin recently described the midnight ride of Paul Revere: "He who warned, uh, the, the British that they weren't gonna be takin' away our arms, uh, by ringin' those bells and, um, makin' sure as he's riding his horse through town to send those warning shots and bells that, uh, we were gonna be secure and we were going to be free—and we were going to be armed." There is but a single reason for including this quote: to give you one final laugh.

988

Sports teams are not the only ones who extort our communities for goodies: big businesses do it to our states all the time.

989

Students should try to obtain their grades from financial credit rating agencies like Standard & Poor's. They will give anyone AAA grades in exchange for a reasonable "incentive." Of course, all these inflated grades would inevitably bring ruin to our country's educational system—just as the specious ratings of mortgage-backed securities crashed the world's financial system in 2008.

990

Before we begin altering the brains of our budding children with psychiatric drugs, we should first try a few parenting courses.

991

To be successful, do not do the things you feel like doing until you have done the necessary things you do not feel like doing.

992

Note how the GOP always agrees that defense spending must be cut—but only after we have slashed everything else (i.e., never).

993

The next time you hear a right-winger talking about the need for shared sacrifice, ask that person to name one significant sacrifice that our government has forced upon millionaires.

994

I want no piece of any additional shared sacrifice: *the wealthy have earned all of it.* Since Reagan became president, the upper class has grown much richer as the lower and middle classes have grown poorer. By my reckoning, we common folk have already made our fair share of sacrifices.

995

All levels of government face severe budget deficits. The lower and middle classes are broke. Only our aristocrats have wealth. Only they can bail out Main Street to jumpstart the economy, yet they refuse to do so. *Hence, to get the funds we need to rescue our country, we have no option but to raise the upper-income tax rates.* It is time for aristocrats to sacrifice. (But they should not worry: in very little time, they will take all their taxes back through their capitalistic maneuvers.)

996

Rep. Paul Ryan sincerely believes that he can "save" Medicare *by dismantling it*, just as the GOP has always believed that it can use similar schemes to save each of the other social programs we value in America.

997

It is not society's responsibility to educate you, for that task is really yours alone.

998

"You need to have a gun," Neal Boortz recently said on his radio show. This popular right-wing commentator who refers to himself as "Mighty Whitey" then continued his vile rant: "And you do in fact need to carry that gun and we need to see some dead [urban] thugs littering the landscape in Atlanta." Boortz's hate speech gives us a taste of the anarchic future that looms ahead. If we cannot reverse the spread of poverty, many more voices will urge us to kill "thugs" with our guns—and in somebody's eyes, *every one of us is a thug*. Consequently, we will all become targets.

999

I must now come out of the closet. To write this book, I had to ruthlessly interrogate all of my thoughts—and this led me to a life-changing discovery: I am an atheist. Since coming to this realization, I am more at peace spiritually than ever before. I know that this public revelation will earn me the hostilities of people who pretend to be Christians, but I make it with the hope that it will encourage other atheists to bravely step forth. As we grow stronger in numbers, the crippling grip of religion will weaken.

1000

All that is "evil" arises from ignorance and greed, and all that is "good" arises from enlightenment and unselfishness. So which side of humanity's ethical struggle will you champion?

Afterword

Within this book, I gave you a thousand of my thoughts. I truly hope they enriched your life. But if you are like me, you enjoy receiving bargains, getting more than you anticipated — and so I wish to offer you more via a piece of advice: *boldly discuss these thoughts with everybody*. The aphorisms I have set in your hands are but seeds that need healthy debate for full cultivation. It can clarify, expand, and multiply each of them. In essence — if you take my advice — this book will become "the gift that keeps on giving."

About the Author

In 1965, when Kenneth Rotar was only nine months old, doctors diagnosed him with spinal muscular atrophy, a form of muscular dystrophy. Though it was unlikely that he would survive much past his teenage years, he has lived a full life with many roles (e.g., poster child, college honors graduate, corporate accountant, political activist, talk radio host, writer, and husband). He has steadily lost nearly all of his muscles and can barely move his limbs or digits; nonetheless, he completed this book of philosophy at the age of 46.

Kenneth is now 49 and is still living with his wife in Madison, Wisconsin, where he is conducting research for his next project.

For more information, visit www.bricksoftruth.com.

General Index of Aphorisms

Made in the USA
Las Vegas, NV
15 March 2022

45670419R10125